Contents

UNIVERSITY OF PLYMOUTH
LIBRARY SERVICES

Item No.   3759277

Class No.   374.42 Com

Contl No.   1 871516 277

WITHDRAWN
FROM
UNIVERSITY OF PLYMOUTH

90 0375927 7

COMPUTERS AND LANGUAGE

Edited by Moira Monteith

intellect

OXFORD, ENGLAND

First Published in 1993 by
Intellect Books
Suite 2, 108/110 London Road, Oxford OX3 9AW

Copyright © 1993 Intellect Ltd.

All rights reserved. No part of this publication may be reproduced,
stored in a retrieval system, or transmitted, in any form or by any
means, electronic, mechanical, photocopying, recording, or otherwise,
without written permission.

Consulting editor: Masoud Yazdani
Copy editor: Cate Foster
Cover design: Mark Lewis

British Library Cataloguing in Publication Data available

ISBN 1-871516-27-7

Printed and bound in Great Britain by Cromwell Press, Wiltshire

Contributors

Chris Breese is the Head of English in Bedwell School in Stevenage Hertfordshire. For the last four years he has been running an experiment to study the effects upon children's writing of unlimited access to word processors. He believes that computer technology could revolutionise the delivery and the processes of education but is not optimistic about the likelihood of adequate financial provision Chris is married with two young children who have taken over his home computer - nearly!

Francis Curtis is a Senior Lecturer at the West Sussex Institute of Higher Education where he is currently co-ordinator for Secondary English in the PGCE. He is interested in the application of Information Technology to the Secondary English Curriculum and is currently working on the effects of typography, especially digital typography, on the reader.

Susan Groundwater-Smith is an Associate Professor in the School of Teacher Education at the University of Technology, Sydney, Australia. She has undertaken a number of research and evaluation studies which have examined the impact of the microcomputer on the school curriculum. Her principal interest is in the microcomputer as a powerful learning tool. More broadly she is concerned with the study of curriculum and evaluation as a set of social practices.

Stephen Marcus PhD is on the faculty of the Graduate School of Education of the University of California, Santa Barbara, USA, where he co-ordinates the California Technology Project/California Writing Project Alliance. He has served on the Commission on Media for the National Council of Teachers of English, and is on the Board of Directors for the organisation's Assembly on Computers and English. He has published widely on the field of computers in education, including 11 software titles, one of which was named in a national survey of teachers' favourite software.

Harry McMahon is Senior Lecturer in Education at the University of Ulster at Coleraine. He began his career as a school science teacher in the early 1960s and moved into teacher training and educational research in 1968. Since then he has worked in the areas of science education, curriculum theory and the development and use of Information Technology in first and third world schools.

Moira Monteith has taught in a variety of schools and Higher Education Institutions in Great Britain and Canada. She is currently head of the Centre for

Information Technology and Business Education in the School of Education at Sheffield Hallam University. Previous publications include books and articles on writing, the application of computers to English and women's education.

Richard Monteith is a freelance consultant and software developer who has taught Information Technology and computer skills to a wide range of students aged from 5 to 75 years.

Bahman Najarian has a PhD in psychology from the University of York, where he is a Visiting Fellow. He is currently teaching and researching at the Department of Education, University of Shahid Chamran, in Ahwaz, Iran.

Bill O'Neill is Lecturer in Education at the University of Ulster at Coleraine. His academic background is in psychology and he has wide experience of teaching in primary schools in the UK and abroad. Currently his work involves the training of primary school teachers, with special focus on language and literacy.

Mike Peacock joined the National Evaluation of TVEI team at the University of Leeds after experience as a journalist and a teacher. His most recent publications present findings from his PhD research into student literacy, particularly the effects and implications of word processing.

Jon Pratt, formerly Head of the English Department at Bushfield Community School, Peterborough, Jon was Project Officer for the PALM(Pupils as Autonomous Learners using Microcomputers) Project in Cambridgeshire from 1989-91. At present he is Senior Adviser with responsibility for project development with the Cambridgeshire Curriculum Agency, part of the Cambridgeshire Inspectorate and Advisory Service

Brent Robinson was a teacher of English and is now University Lecturer in Information Technology in Education and Fellow of Hughes Hall, Cambridge. He was a Co-ordinator of the Communications Collaborative Project funded by the National Council for Educational Technology, and National Co-ordinator for The Distant Muse Electronic Communications Project funded by the Paul Hamlyn Foundation, the Arts Council of Great Britain and the National Council for Educational Technology.

Chris Warren became a teacher in 1977. He moved to Derbyshire in 1980, where in 1984, he began to explore the role of Information Technology in the English classroom. He joined the Derbyshire CAL (Computer Assisted Learning) Project and three years later was appointed Advisory Teacher for IT and English. He has worked intensively on simulations and creative uses of Electronic Mail. A member of the NATE New Technologies Committee, he is now Curriculum Director for Communications and Language at Buxton Community School.

Noel Williams was educated at King's College Cambridge and Sheffield University. He is now a Principal Lecturer at Sheffield Hallam University where he runs the Communication and Information Research Group. He is author/editor of ten books in the field of communication and computing.

1
Introduction

Moira Monteith

As a child I was excited by reading. It took me into areas I could not go to otherwise and particularly, as a girl, to male areas of sport and adventure. In fact I was a typical case-book example of the kind my teachers, and those I later taught with, liked to use to encourage reading. Those teachers perhaps overvalued novels and plays and underestimated comics and what I called 'real' stories.

The chapters in this book are all real stories with a practical dimension. Harry McMahon and Bill O'Neill begin their contribution: 'This is a story about storying'. Maybe I am excited reading these pieces because I grew up as a print kid and not a computer kid. They give me that bite that all good reading does, the sense of reliving someone else's experience, of wanting to copy or alter that experience myself, even if only feebly. I would like therefore, as editor, to set the context of this book as I see it. The contributors clearly have views of their own.

One appropriate approach to computers in education is to view them as change agents. This approach implies developmental change; neither change for the sake of change nor that of the old adage: *the more things change the more they are the same.* Susan Groundwater-Smith indicates the potential of this approach when she talks about writing: '...using the microcomputer as a writing tool has enabled us to more fully apprehend the complexity of this human action'. Examining our use of computers helps us to understand our teaching and learning practices. It throws into relief our attitudes to learning situations and either encourages a new response or a shock of dismay and anxiety. Microcomputers bring with them the possibility of pedagogical reform as commonplace practices change to accommodate them. I hope this book will help readers to develop their own reassessments and promote some serenity rather than dismay in response to change.

I believe that most schools in the UK have now reached the end of the pre-change period, a time of first reactions common to us all when faced with new technology. We might take up this new tool but use it only in the ways we used the old one without wanting to explore its new capabilities, or else have it in the room to show it's there but use it as little as possible. Only a few people ever wished to hide away computers along with other little used equipment in dusty cupboards, but they did often put them in places where it was comparatively difficult to use them, for example in locked rooms with only one key or draughty corridors where the pupils were away from the rest of the classroom activity.

Comparable to the physical placing of the computer were the uses to which it was put. For instance, some pupils were allowed to use the computer as a treat, a reward for having done the hard work on some other task. Others were sent in rotation for drill work on, for example, spelling exercises which although they might be quite cheerful exercises in themselves, also meant the pupil was separated from the class rather in the way people might be sent to take medicine. Other pupils used the word-processor to make the 'fair copy' which would go up on the wall or be put in the class magazine; or they made titles in very large print which could go above the class work on the wall.

It would be foolish to underestimate the major organisational problems involved with the use of computers in our present classroom system. Teachers frequently have little or no close technical support and any proposed use of the computer must include practical time/space considerations which usually take up valuable energy. Nevertheless teachers are making considerable progress in implementing the application of computers to pupils' learning activities. Advice on strategies for such use is becoming more widespread, often owing much to advisory teachers and Local Education Authority (LEA) training programmes. We seem therefore to be at the stage where the effects of such implementation need to be assessed while at the same time we retain a sense of momentum. New developments are taking place - such as the new CD ROM initiatives - so that teachers are aware that new demands will be made upon their current competence. Trainee teachers are being asked to 'evaluate the ways in which the use of Information Technology (IT) changes the nature of teaching and learning'(DES Circular 24/89).

A focus on classroom use of computers causes us to reconsider factors such as classroom behaviour and management. Computers may well require a change in the teaching role. Teachers sometimes feel that the role of facilitator is disappointing and does not always stimulate the use of their full potential or skills in teaching. On the other hand, an authoritarian model may not develop all pupils' potentials very effectively and is certainly difficult to maintain when a teacher cannot be expert in every computer program or a wide range of hardware. The National Curriculum sensibly advocates the teacher as practising exemplar in certain fields. For example: *Programme of Study for Key Stage 1, English:* 'Pupils should see adults writing. Teachers should write alongside pupils, sharing and talking about their writing so that the range of uses of writing is brought out.' Such a model might go some way to meeting problems that have come to the fore with the growth of new technology in the classroom. As teachers in this field we must inevitably feel less than expert on occasion. We will meet with pupils who, with sophisticated systems at home, may become more expert than any teacher in the school, even the ablest technology teacher.

We need a role more profound than that of facilitator yet not that of 'experts' undermined by feelings of inadequacy as to our own knowledge and skill. Our expertise as teachers lies in developing pupils' and students' potential and managing stratagems for achieving this. Certain pupils may have expert knowledge with specific programs or even computer systems but will need help applying their skills. We must therefore take a new look at 'mixed ability'. Pupils with expert knowledge (not necessarily the brightest in the class) should not be discouraged. It seems also to be recognised that most of these young experts with sophisticated systems are male. Teachers need to manage and disseminate the collective expertise available instead of attempting to be the fount of all wisdom and knowledge.

It seems timely to publish a book which deals specifically with one subject area - computers and language - but considers it within a continuum of experience and application. The National Curriculum may have the effect of slotting pupils into competencies and age phases where IT expertise may not fit entirely happily unless we emphasise the continuum of schooling. Our contributors have worked with a number of different projects and different age phases yet all deal with interrelated aspects of computer usage. The themes interlock. It is a collaborative book rather than the work of one individual or other people's work seen from my viewpoint. Some publishers are alleged to shy away from books with multiple authors on the grounds that the chapters are disconnected and readers do not like such books. It is true that not all the chapters may seem entirely relevant to each reader but such a book is responsive to a reader's concerns. You know where you are. Each writer signals his or her starting point very clearly. You can indeed pick and choose though I hope you will read some sections which may not seem at first entirely pertinent to you. At a recent conference (September 1991) held at Sheffield City Polytechnic where one of the major aims was to build links between schools and higher education, a number of participants commented favourably on these links in their evaluations. As Rosetta McLeod wrote: 'I do hope that as a result of the conference ways can be found of bringing staff from secondary and tertiary education closer together'. Many of us would like to include primary staff as well in such a liaison. In the past schools have often been seen as fodder for educational research. New technology can encourage collaboration within a working relationship.

Interaction and collaboration are important features of language behaviour. Their combination has become one of the significant themes of this book. All contributors assume a more highly emphasised interaction generated at a number of levels: between individuals, between writer and computer, the generations-old inter-relationships between author and text, writers and teacher, as well as between the various media involved. Susan Groundwater-Smith begins by looking at the whole question of individual writing versus collaborative writing. She states that writing is a struggle. It is also the most individualised of the activities undertaken during our education and the most highly valued. Writing serves a number of interests which she defines as technical, practical or hermeneutic and emancipatory. She offers a challenge to the orthodoxy of individualism and suggests that writing collaboratively requires more debate and research about 'languaging'. Collaborative writing requires complex negotiation while word-processing allows both the generation and the management of text. Traditionally society has valued the art object produced individually above work produced by a group. Collective meaning-making is inconsistent with the assessment processes employed in our educational institutions. She indicates the importance and relevance of talk to writing and quotes as an example a discussion by a group of girls before they wrote to pupils in an American school via electronic mail. She also gives an example of ten-year-old pupils debating most effectively on how to summarise their presentation. She reveals the rigorous collaborative processes necessary to achieve an agreed meaning and states that this process should be considered at least as important as programming activities. All texts are influenced by other texts in the environment around us but collaborative texts provide better opportunities for making our reasonings explicit and give rise to a different writing experience.

Stephen Marcus asks the question which is becoming pertinent to us all: 'Who is learning what, from which technology, with what other effects on learning and behaviour?' He is concerned with the manner in which computer technology is changing the nature of text as well as the process of decoding our thought. He starts by giving a series of useful definitions on new tools: videotext, where information does not go into you but you go into it, hypertext where the mind 'operates by association', the hypertext environment and interactive fiction. Throughout the discussion he comments on the appropriate software available. Some is generally available in the UK, for example, *Guide* and *HyperCard*; other programs are more accessible in the USA. However, the American scene gives us a strong indication of paths we shall probably follow in the UK. Stephen focuses on *HyperCard*, 'the Swiss Army knife of educational software', and his own work as he began to use it. He then discusses a variety of uses to which *HyperCard* has been put and indicates the great potential for collaborative work and individual creative development. He ends with some fascinating evidence that suggests that different language users and different genders may employ different approaches to organising knowledge. Sophisticated tools are coming which help all groups of individuals to develop their knowledge base effectively so that we will not be straitjacketed by having to take one route only.

Jon Pratt begins his section by looking at the theoretical basis for the concept of autonomous learning. He draws on his experience of working and researching with teachers on the PALM Project and outlines some of their conclusions. He believes that computers introduce 'significant cultural differences in children's attitudes to learning.' As teachers we may have to relearn our own attitudes. A realignment of classroom organisational patterns becomes necessary as old orthodoxies, for instance that of the 'resident expert', disappear. Jon Pratt thinks that action research is a valuable method to use in teachers' continuing education. He ends with a telling comment from a teacher's research journal where she discovered: 'the change of emphasis from pupil/teacher relationship to that of a team radiated into all areas of the curriculum'.

Chris Breese has written his chapter in the form of a letter to his Headteacher. It concerns the project he undertook for three years in which each child in a Year 7 class, that is, aged eleven to twelve years, was able to use a laptop computer in English. He records their increased motivation and considers that the support of both teacher as 'language consultant' at the significant time of composition and that of word-processor in terms of ease of use and positive encouragement to redraft are both vital to writing. He then puts into perspective the difficulties of the time factor when it comes to covering all the work needed for the syllabus. If pupils spend a great deal of time redrafting and thus harnessing the power of the word-processor how will they get through the syllabus? He ends by making three proposals: (1) that the school should discuss a 'writing across the curriculum' policy; (2) that pupils' access to computers should be improved; and (3), that the syllabus demands should be reconsidered and co-operative ways of dealing with the written work devised. He emphasises how computer technology and curriculum design go hand in hand.

Mike Peacock and Bahman Najarian have written a highly practical paper which is also a serious piece of academic research. It carries the virtues of both approaches. Whereas the rest of the contributors may seem carried away occasionally by their own enthusiasm and that generated by their pupils and students, Mike and Najarian bring us down to ground. Their title is 'What is important in writing?' and they maintain there is an attitudinal change in the way pupils think of writing when they have become accustomed to the use of word-processors. Mike and Najarian believe it is difficult to substantiate short-term improvements in children's writing when using word-processors. Accounts of usage often ignore additional teacher assistance alongside the benefits of word-processing and the effect of print itself on any assessors. They suggest that word-processing children may be adopting 'an attitude to writing characteristic of "expert" writers'.

Therefore they set up a project 'to examine whether experienced pupil users of word-processors display signs of any difference in attitude to the surface, the compositional, or the contextual features of their writing relative to their handwriting contemporaries'. The project involved 135 pupils at three secondary schools. The research comes up with some very interesting findings. Pupils have a more 'nonchalant' attitude to writing when using a word-processor and are less concerned with the secretarial features of their writing or indeed those connected with its meaning. This could have very positive outcomes but there is an important caveat. It is vital that teachers encourage students to use the technology more effectively.

Brent Robinson also considers collaborative writing, in the instances cited using both electronic communication and 'expert' writers. He sets the context for the specific project with which he was involved. The project was designed in part to give a 'very clear sense of narrative direction and a time scale for the activity', factors which had not always been present in previous trials with electronic mail and perhaps had led to some projects petering out as interest died. The first project, funded by the Eastern Arts Association and the National Council for Educational Technology (NCET) decided to focus on the epistolary form of narrative. Children from six schools became role-play explorers who communicated back to a professional writer in the guise of a bedridden archaeologist. In the second project children were role-play prisoners in solitary confinement who communicated with another prisoner who was again a professional writer. Brent explores the values of such a project and comments on some of the problems uncovered, such as the distancing of the writer from the pupils and the rejection (in terms of publication) of some of their work. Subsequently teacher training students took part in similar schemes using electronic mail, corresponding with children in schools. Brent also considers the potential tension between the teachers' expectations as regards language use and the more informal use prevalent among e-mail users. He concludes with a review of the possibilities inherent in a combination of mail media.

Chris Warren looks at computer-based simulations. He discusses both the practical use of a machine-controlled news dissemination, which leaves the teacher free to interreact with the pupils, and the seductiveness of the process in which the participants become more and more prepared to suspend disbelief as the activity continues. He goes on to consider the impact of computer-based information flow on language and thought processes represented by language. In these simulations it is important that the computer is an information source and **not** the primary focus of attention. The main activity goes on away from the computer and Chris gives some riveting examples of language use resulting from the use of *Hijack*. Having observed the *Murder* simulation a number of times he is able to generalise from his observations. He believes the simulations give opportunities for collaborative thought as well as talk, and outlines what he has observed as stages in the collaborative thought process. He suggests some interesting analogies with other groups, for example that of families touching photographs as they look at them together in a group. He examines the function of questions as a means of arriving at group conclusions. His acute observation gives rise to general theoretical points of great interest to classroom teachers and anyone concerned with group dynamics.

Francis Curtis opens up another dimension of the vital debate concerning language and computers by looking at their impact on language itself and therefore how we conceptualise the world around us, the metaphors generated by computer use and the ways in which we describe these machines. The significance of metaphor in this context has already been touched on by Jon Pratt at the beginning of his chapter. It is evident that we do seek to make concrete our use of computers by talking about toolboxes and palettes, desktops and windows. It seems no accident that we also have the development of object-oriented programming languages which act as an interface between systems and programmers and systems and users. Francis begins with quotations from Dickens and an Apricot manual, both heavily metaphorical. He looks at the relationships between language and computers in education by exploring the characteristics of computer discourse in theory and in classroom practice. He examines the changes brought about by the computer in English teaching and those likely to be brought about by the National Curriculum requirements. The dichotomy in our relationship with the computer - an extension of ourselves or a piece of technology functioning separately from ourselves - is emphasised. He goes on to analyse clusters of metaphors and concludes there are five prominent categories, those that are concerned with transport or merchandise plus those that can be described as military, household or organic. He makes the point that as users we can become confused between our expectations of computer use and reality. An actual classroom situation where he is discussing computer discourse with a Year 10 class is cited. He gives examples of their insights and concludes with a general statement as to the general importance of metaphor in influencing our culture.

Noel Williams introduces the notion of postwriting tools at the editing stage of writing. We are often very aware of the advantages of word-processing itself but perhaps do not think what other facilities are available, whether we need any or all of them and what effect they might have on our writing. Noel looks at the various functions of such tools, for instance, readability, pattern matching (for spell checkers, grammar, indices of style, frequency of items, comparisons with ideals). He then goes on to evaluate the programs which carry out these specific functions. He considers the variable nature of their use and their benefits to teachers and students. If teachers are freed from more mechanical tasks they will be asked to meet more sophisticated queries. Students, particularly when engaged in writing one variety of text, for example report writing, may well find the use of postwriting tools extremely helpful. Teachers can begin to address the issue of computer help not just in terms of word-processed text but of subsequent help before the final version is published. Noel has given us a remarkably accurate survey of this field.

Harry McMahon and Bill O'Neill focus on the significance of storying to the human mind and aim to 'subvert technology to educational objectives'. They compare the way in which the pen and paper and printing cultures bind a story into a linear form whereas hypertext allows links and connections to be made between aspects and elements of a story. These links which occur in a non-linear framework are readily conceptualised by children who quickly develop the ability to create complex non-linear structures. They assert that drawings have become integral aspects of the meaning-making process in their hypermedia projects.

They approve of a critical analysis of new technology as it enters educational use. *HyperCard*, for instance, is not a pre-packaged computer solution to educational problems but they give positive evidence of its creative use by teachers and pupils which is highly interactional. Harry first produced 'a graphical, animated adventure' about Harry's dog, Ginny. In company with another writer, Orla O'Neill, aged seven, dialogue 'bubbles' were designed to encourage the development of literacy along with graphic work. After the first use of the Bubble Dialogue tool Harry and Bill investigated multimedia in general and *HyperCard* in particular to see if they could be used by groups in classrooms. They are quite sure that it is the quality of interaction between pupils and teacher that ensures quality learning and not the computer applications in themselves.

The bubble dialogue 'exploits the natural tendency of children to actively participate in dialogue...' It 'draws on the interactional turn taking aspect of conversation'. It moves children 'from talk through reflection to literacy', 'from the informal language of the home and playground to the more formal language of school to the increasingly abstract language of written text'. It also allows them to express their understanding of private and public worlds. They give an example of an ending where the use of more than one medium reinforces the narrative impact:

the crocodile is heard munching up the hero as the reader unravels the text and pictures.

Moira and Richard Monteith end the book by giving a deliberately practical summary of three projects using *HyperCard* with classes in infant, junior and secondary schools. The underlying aim of all three projects was to discover if their classroom experience could be replicated fairly easily by other teachers. Not only did this seem to be true but they found that pupils developed language skills in quite definite and original ways. It is true that the pupils had extra attention during the time they were working with computers, so this should be kept in mind when evaluating the results, as Mike Peacock has pointed out. However, it is also clear that these projects resulted in different collaborative end products than could have been achieved by other means. The books and stacks constructed by the pupils could not have been completed without the use of this software. It also seems highly likely that the relationship between a variety of texts and illustrations realised by the pupils in their work was enhanced by this particular use.

Because readers are as important as writers in the collaborative process I would appreciate any comments you would like to send me, either about the contributions in this book or your own experience or what you would like to see included in any future similar collection.

2
Beyond the individual: collaborative writing and the microcomputer

Susan Groundwater-Smith

Writing is a struggle. It is wresting often inchoate 'ideas' from the mind and rendering them in a form accessible to others. Schutz (1982) has characterised writing as 'catching the world of inner experience in the net of language' (p.130). The struggle is a silent one. The writer generates and discards one notion after another and may not have composed even one sentence, one phrase, one word in the space of time taken to think a host of thoughts. The writing is the result of an interior 'dialogue'; a kind of purposeful arguing with oneself or an imaginary listener. Each argument arises out of others which have been made before in the speculative head of the writer.

Of all of the activities in which people engage in educational settings, writing is the most individualised, and in the end, the most valorised. It is the writing which is rewarded, the outcome of a silent and often painful struggle. The culture of individualism is constantly reinforced as schools, colleges and universities elicit and evaluate written products. In these contexts the ubiquitous, and singular author, contrary to Barth's assertions (1975), is alive and well.

No doubt some readers of this piece will wish to argue that their institutions are much more interested in group processes and group outcomes. However, in the Australian context at least the kinds of assessment and accountability procedures which currently prevail drive course designers back upon individual tasks and assignments.

All this is not to suppose that writing is exclusively instrumental and cognitive. It is at the same time an expressive and cultural activity (Faigley, 1986) which is not only social in its instigation and context but social in its various outcomes. The individual who writes is both a constituent of the culture of which he or she is a member and reflexively constitutes that culture. In other words, societal norms act upon the writer, while the writer acts upon the societal norms.

Clearly, writing serves a number of different knowledge interests. The purpose may be purely instrumental, as a means to an end. The knowledge interest here is a **technical** one, although the task may range in difficulty from something as simple as setting down the method for boiling an egg to explaining the complex bio-technic procedure for cloning a cell, or drafting a constitution for a newly formed government. Such purposes it must be remembered are not value-free, although they are often represented as such. A second knowledge interest is of a **practical/**

hermeneutic kind, in which the writing project is associated with the description and interpretation of events and phenomena. A third, and perhaps the most challenging knowledge interest is of an illuminative, even **emancipatory** kind, which serves to crystallise insights and understandings about the very nature of our human condition. The composition here may be a narrative, a poem, a philosophical treatise. Irrespective of genre, it is writing which is liberatory, taking us beyond current norms and conventions. Potentially, a written text may encompass all three knowledge interests corresponding to the task which the writer has set herself or himself.

The means of producing a range of written tests, in institutional settings such as schools and universities, has been the matter of vigorous, even polemical debate.

Arguments have revolved around, inter alia, providing models of instruction, having access to the conventions of different generic forms and the ownership of topics (Christie, 1987; Scardamalia & Paris, 1985; Turbill, 1988). The fulcrum, however, has been uncontested, that writing is an individual activity, but simultaneously (and paradoxically) it is a signifying practice, adhering to strict institutionally and historically derived codes.

Even as I write this paper, although an individual, I am bound by the conventions of academic prose. The expectation of most of my audience is that I shall not be too prolix, too anecdotal or too colourful. On the other hand, if I were writing for the popular press, outlining the use of microcomputers in developing children's writing, this paper would be cast as too abstract and lacking practical advice. This code would have shifted. It is the intention of this paper to mount a challenge to the orthodoxy of individualism which I have argued is so prevalent and to propose that writing collaboratively in our educational institutions requires a fuller theorising of 'languaging'. Furthermore I wish to demonstrate that use of the microcomputer as a writing tool has enabled us to apprehend more fully the complexity of this human action.

If individual writing is a personal struggle, then collaborative writing is an interpersonal contest. For two or more writers to make meaning which satisfies each of them, the negotiation is complex and socially mediated. Writing is no longer a separate language entity, resulting from an isolated activity. It is part of a whole languaging process, oral communication, dramaturgical action and the relating of self to others. Each writer must draw the attention of her or his peers to the reasonings underpinning: the selection of a word or phrase; the juxtaposition of ideas and arguments; the raising and resolution of a particular conundrum; the rejection of alternative voices .... Daiute (1986) in discussing the work of two young writers engaged in a collaborative process indicated that it is not merely a matter of two heads being better than one:

> Explicit negotiations over plot options should lead to the most complex inner dialoguing process, and certain pairs of students benefited from such discussion. Nevertheless, students also benefit from hearing each other compose out loud and trying out alternatives together, even if they do not discuss the pros and cons of alternatives in detail (pp. 405-406).

Before discussing more fully the nature of collaborative writing, I wish now to explore the function of the microcomputer as a writing tool within the context of multiple authorship. It is not by chance that when we speak of writing using a microcomputer, we generically speak of 'word processing'. For the writing application goes far beyond the function of some kind of an electronic typewriter which would enable the mechanical creation of letters on a page. Word processing does just what its name implies. It allows both the **generation** and the **management** of text. The users can 'process' the text by shaping and re-shaping it. A number of versions can be developed and saved in a more accessible form than crude, cut and pasted missives. The microcomputer allows the writers greater control of the composing process; with greater control comes an increased opportunity for experimentation. Editing can go beyond merely attending to surface changes in spelling and vocabulary and can lead to an accumulated re conceptualising of the written piece.

Of course, all of this is available to the individual writer, but it is particularly facilitating for several writers working collaboratively. At the point of utterance, changes can be made and new paths taken. The high visibility of the monitor allows the merging text to be easily apprehended and discussed. Several hard copies can be made so that writers may reflect and revise before coming together again.

It is not always the case that collaborative writing with the microcomputer means that the product is exclusively generated while at a workstation. Lunniss (1987), in reporting upon a South Australian action research project using microcomputers as a writing tool observed :

> Writing was easier to discuss and re-drafting easier to accomplish. Many students to whom writing was often a real chore enjoyed writing with the word processor. It gave them a neat copy, both on the screen and in hard copy, adding to their self esteem. It encouraged them to re-draft because it wasn't a matter of painfully re-writing pages of text. It could be fun, 'a real buzz' as one Year 8 student put it. Perhaps more importantly, this willingness to re-draft was not restricted to the screen ..... Time was spent re-working printouts of drafts in preparation for the next time using the word processor (pp.22-23).

In considering ourselves as writers, my husband and I commenced a paper, (Groundwater-Smith & Smith 1987) on collaborative writing thus:

> We know each other well, we share a marriage, a home, two children and a dog. We have talked about children's writing over many years; indeed, have argued and disputed problems related to the process. At this moment one of us is composing, that is discovering an understanding which is being electronically stored and can be readily retrieved and revised. The other will later read the piece, argue, delete, add to it, elaborate, dispute ... We shall talk about the writing in the car, at the table, while washing the dog. More changes

will be made. We shall debate about register, the audience, the metaphors we use, the ideologies we represent. But the piece in the end will be seamless. Although each one of us will be able to identify some components as our own thoughts they will have been transmuted, the form and substance of the original idea will have been not merely modified by the addition of a phrase, or a full stop, it will itself have changed. Fresh understandings and more cogent formulations will have emerged (p.2).

But, the argument goes, there is in spite of our assertion of 'seamlessness', a problem of 'unity'. A single authored piece has the authenticity of being a wholly owned piece, of having the integrity and coherence which one mind brings to the writing. Honouring such individualism is deeply embedded in our western 'high' cultural tradition. Imagine a poem written by two or more writers, a play which is the result of a collaborative process, a painting produced by several artists, a piano concerto or an opera composed by a group of musicians, a ballet choreographed by the dancers themselves. This may well do for popular culture, for musicals, for rock bands and the makers of soap operas, but is not applauded and valued in the same manner as the highly individualistic art object.

This individualism is not the case in all cultures, nor has it been the case in all eras of Western culture. Aboriginal painters, for example, eschew signing their work as individuals, they acknowledge individual craft skills only in so much as one may paint one part of the work while others may be apprenticed to produce minor sections. But the knowledge of **the meaning** is collective in prospect and retrospect and it is that which is precious. The products may be commodified by acquisitive and wealthy non-Aboriginal collectors and galleries, but to the creators they are ephemeral. It is the collective meaning making which has mattered. Singing the land, for Aboriginal peoples is more than the song. Song lines, drawn across the land, signify its symbolic history, taking account of both the past and the present and the inexorable connections between.

As I have already suggested, in our schools and our universities the notion of collective meaning-making is inconsistent with the processes of assessment and credentialling. In the end the examination is taken by the individual. The marks are individually assigned. The individual is confirmed as one who has succeeded or otherwise in learning what the institution has tried to teach. To change all of this would be a formidable task indeed, much effort and little effect. Does this mean, then, that to argue for collaborative work in schools and universities, specifically collaborative writing using microcomputers, is little more than a tactic for sharing scarce resources with no intrinsic value attached? To this question I would voice a vehement 'no!'. For in spite of our taken-for-granted assessment practices, with their means/ends emphasis, there is another learning going on and this is a learning about and through communicative action. If schools, colleges and universities are to be more than teaching shops, then the project of engaging in collective meaning-making, with all of the attendant implications, should have the highest of priorities.

The role of the microcomputer in all of this is not serendipitous. The penetration of the technology into educational settings has been significant and may be regarded as a curriculum innovation in its own right. Microcomputers bring with them the possibility of pedagogical reform as commonplace practices change to accommodate them. As Kemmis (1987) has observed:

> .... developments in computing are not merely changing the technology of education while leaving educational processes themselves unchanged; they are also creating opportunities for changing education itself (p.272).

This concept can be best demonstrated by taking examples from practice. During 1987, I had the opportunity to take part in an evaluation of an electronic mail project managed by Bridget Somekh at the Cambridge Institute of Education (Groundwater-Smith & Somekh, 1987). Briefly, modems were installed in schools in Cambridge, Peterborough and Newcastle in the UK, and in Massachusetts in the USA. Teachers were encouraged to form social professional networks in order that they determine, collectively, a writing curriculum which would take into account communication between schools and between countries. Several mini-projects ensued, among them a writing link with Israel; a progressive story writing activity; a between-schools literature exchange and a school-based electronic pen friend scheme.

Part of the evaluation task was to examine the following questions with respect to collaborative writing:

1. How do learners collectively make meaning?

2. For whom, and by whom, is the meaning constructed?

3. What is the worthwhileness of a project such as this?

The making of meaning, in the instances which were observed, was clearly a complex, socially mediated process. The writers were required, not only to explain and argue for their own contribution to the shared text, but also to take account of their co-writers' arguments and explanations, while, at the same time, considering the needs of the readers, who were often unseen and unknown. Mehan *et al* (1984) claim the microcomputer makes possible a new social organisation for literacy; I would add it also provides a powerful context for oracy. The shared oral discourses which are engendered by the strategic demands of the task constitute, in my view, a significant benefit equal to the written product itself.

Consider the following exchange between a group of adolescent girls preparing to write their first letter to Massachusetts :

Lucy: Well, I see the school as large, white, easy, relaxed ....there'd be no uniforms.

Becky: I wonder if they're snobby? If they're stuck up.

Claire: It might be a bit rough. They might have a drug problem.

Becky: There'd be black kids. Some black teachers too. There aren't any black teachers in Cambridge (this was said with some scorn, Becky is, herself, a vivacious and ebullient black girl). I imagine the teachers to be young ...

Claire: I think there'd be more to do in the evenings. The school would have more sport, more sporting facilities ...

Lucy: I think they'd be able to get off lessons more easily.

Becky: Yeah, I wonder if they bunk off, visit friends, you know, layabout, go down town. I bet they think we're all clever, living in Cambridge and that.

Lucy: I don't know. Because it's funny, in a way they're more strict - singing the anthem, saluting the flag. It's like the Brownies really.

Daiute (1985) has observed that writers need to talk to themselves about the process of creating text. These young writers **had** to talk to each other. They needed to discuss and clarify the notions they held about the audience in relation to their writing. The voice and address questions are far more explicit and for the sensitive teacher offer opportunities to gain insights into the ways that young writers are constructing their audience. For example, when the first chapters of the progressive story were received by teenagers in Cambridge, the students' initial reaction was not to deal with the substance, but to deal with identifying and understanding the writers in order to find ways of validating the material and, reciprocally, to perceive the needs of the readers as the next piece of text was generated. 'Are they boys or girls?' 'How do we know if they're **really thick** or just acting that way?'

All too often, in educational settings, there is a presumption that the writers know their audience and consequently believe they know what it is that their audience wants to read. The audience demands on the text are consequently coercive, and so are distorting. When the audience is less familiar then genuine attempts need to be made to communicate in undistorted ways. Here is a real possibility for change in the pedagogical practices.

Consider the following. One of the classes in the electronic mail project was engaged in a link with an Israeli school. The teacher had invited into her class a Jewish mother to tell of the Festival of Purim. So animated were the children by the presentation that they set about making a series of masks representing characters in the ancient story. The children subsequently decided to display these in the school foyer with an accompanying explanation of the characters' roles and their relationships both one with the other and with the unfolding events of the narrative. In the episode which follows Melody was concerned with tying the characters together. At the behest of David and Deborah she had entered 'Mordichai was an old and wise Jewish man. He had a niece called Esther'. On her own initiative she added 'You will read about her below'.

David: This is starting to sound like a magazine story. (Parodying Melody) 'you will read about her below'.

Melody: No need to be nasty. It's to organise ... to see. They now know what will be coming.

Deborah: That's fair David. Melody's right. Now we have to write about bowing to Haman.

David: Alright - How about 'Mordichai did not think he should bow down . . .'

(Melody keyed this in.)

Deborah: Stop. What do you mean **'think'**? He **knew** he shouldn't bow. It was the law.

David: It's the same thing.

Deborah: No it isn't. Thinking means you've got choices. I think I'll watch football ... I think I'll go to the markets ... Mordichai had no choices. He **knew** because it was the **law**.

David: I see. But if we say all that it will be too hard for people reading it. What about ... what about...

Melody: (Having deleted the last sentence.) Just keep it simple: 'Mordichai did not bow to Haman' ...

David: But we should mention the law.

Deborah: Take out the full stop and say something like 'because of his religion'.

David: His Jewish religion.

Melody: That's right, that's right now.

Here we have ten-year-old children examining a profound philosophical question: What is the difference between conjecture and absolute authority? The textual modifications are not merely surface editing. They are the result of children making and strengthening judgements in the sense of knowledge building in a consensual and democratic fashion as proposed by Stenhouse (1983): 'An educational programme (of worth) ... involves the formidable problem of expressing knowledge in those forms and activities which both invite and strengthen the judgements of the learner.' (p.166).

Clearly here we do not have a writing stage, followed by a talking stage. The two processes of oracy and literacy are interwoven in a communal, and often convivial way. During a national evaluation of the Australian Commonwealth Schools' Commission's Computer Education Programme my co-researchers and myself undertook a number of intensive case studies (Bigum *et al.* 1987). At one school, 'Hilltop College', I found an interesting and valuable application which took an adventure game *Flowers of Crystal* and generated from it a complex, collaborative writing task. Pupils were required, as they played the game in pairs, to jot down critical decisions and the reasons for the decisions taken. Afterwards, they wrote a radio script with each playing a protagonist in the adventure. The teacher explained his encouragement to edit and refine the text in this way:

> '... then I said: 'You do something the computer can't do, and that means take another perspective - write from another point of view.' The kids started doing that. The slow ones found that very difficult. ... what I decided to do was to encourage editing. On the computer we have this beautiful optical pen. With it we can just take out entire paragraphs or change the order of sentences or place inserts into the story and put the story into the shape we want. There's no need to re-write entire stories and by using this the girls can see that they can start changing their stories. The beauty of it is that it gets rid of the problem of constantly rewriting. Once the story is written (as a first draft) many students believe it is done: it is finished ... there is a lot of blood, sweat and tears in creating a story. They would say: 'I am not going to cut it up and start again because it is finished' and consequently they were producing substandard work, not all, some were very good. They would either get the story right the first time or they had the persistence to go on and edit and re-edit. But the slower child who put in the hard labour to get that story down on paper says 'why have I got to take it away and redo it?' So the computer takes this labour thing out and writing stories becomes a thing of the imagination' (Bigum *et al..* 1987 p. 92).

Incidentally, the radio scripts which the girls produced were then recorded. The microcomputers were further used to generate music and sound effects. Collaboration moved beyond the work of the pupils and became an across-the-curriculum activity with the school's English and Music Departments working closely together - a significant innovation at the secondary school level. In effect, what began as a simple exercise confined to one medium, burgeoned into a multi-channel, multi-media enterprise.

Primary schools, typically, have had much greater organisational flexibility than have secondary schools with their separate faculties, each responsible for a 'discrete' area of the curriculum (as if that were possible). I recently observed, while supervising the practicum at a primary school in metropolitan Sydney, several children working in across-age pairs using three microcomputers at the back of a classroom. Older children were called 'writing tutors' and assisted younger writers by asking them questions as their stories unfolded. The stimulus material was Allsburg's *The Mysteries of Harris Burdick,* a series of strange, captioned drawings, for which the stories had disappeared. The younger children were developing narratives around selected pictures. While we may not wish to propose that this is collaborative writing in the form of joint authorship, none-the-less, the resulting text was composed out of the interaction. What was particularly noteworthy was the time devoted to the activity. The children in the writing group had all of the morning while other children in the class went about a series of different tasks. Again, in secondary schools, it is difficult to have such long periods of time available for one activity, especially as microcomputers tend to be located in rooms assigned for 'computing' with significant competition for classtime bookings.

The contexts in which microcomputers are used have significant impact upon the way in which they are used. In a recent study, concerned with the construction of computer literacy and girls (Crawford *et al..* 1989) it was found that most computers, in the secondary schools surveyed (106 in all), were located in computer rooms and that these were mainly managed by teachers from the mathematics department. Access to the computer room was invariably by time-tabled slots, with humanities departments gaining significantly less access than maths/computing programmes. Consider the following scenario:

> Access to the computer room was noted as a problem as bookings needed to be made to fit in exactly with a given part in a unit of work and this sometimes could not be determined precisely. The computer room itself is also physically isolated from most other faculties in the school. Its nearest staffroom and classrooms are all located in the mathematics department (Crawford *et al.* 1989 p. 34).

Under such conditions it is not surprising to find a kind of 'computer culture' prevails in which programming, as a maths activity dominated by boys, is valued as 'power usage' while word processing is at best regarded as data entry. Writing as a serious, intellectual activity does not compete with the technical demands of programming. There was little evidence, in the study, of the kinds of collaborative writing discussed above. Even less in evidence was the notion that pupils could use the microcomputers in unsupervised ways.

As Smith, in Groundwater-Smith & Smith (1987) noted, when adolescents worked collaboratively with microcomputers outside the surveillance of the teacher the computer itself became a kind of 'silent chairperson'. Reporting on the Comberton project (Adams & Smith, 1987) Smith suggested that pupils come to play a number of different roles: 'leader, grammarian, speller, entertainer, technician, stylist, keyboard operator, trouble-shooter, storyteller etc.' (p.14). He argued that in sorting out these roles with all their attendant asides and debates, the very presence of the computer terminal acts as a focus, as a catalyst for deliberation, for problem solving as well as a 'silent chairperson'. The interpersonal orientation of the collaborative task was highly valued by the participants. As one pupil, Brian, put it:

> If you're working with ... talking to other people ... you can find out their ideas ... so you've got more of an idea of what people's opinions are. With strict lessons you are liable to learn more - but less about what other people's opinions are ... At first we were anxious (about being left to our own devices) but then we got to know each other more in the group ... what our feelings were about what we were doing (Groundwater-Smith & Smith 1987 p.16).

If significant difficulties are faced when encouraging collaborative writing and the use of the microcomputer in secondary schools, how much more problematic is it to propose such multi-functional action at the tertiary level? The nature of the highly individualised credentials which tertiary institutions bestow upon their graduates means that rarely are undergraduates faced with collaborative assignments of any magnitude. Paradoxically, once in the work force, most graduates will be required to work co-operatively and collegially.

I would like to anecdotally report that in the BEd (primary) course at the University of Sydney which I co-ordinated for some years, we have made some attempt to overcome this reluctance to set assignments requiring collaborative enquiry and subsequent writing. Students working in pairs and threes undertook a semester's observation in a given school. They then presented an account of the school's curriculum practices and were encouraged to write this using the microcomputing facilities of the faculty. It would seem that those who used the facilities produced a more coherent, integrated report than those who did not. Even in the third year of a degree it was clear that some students who produced hand-written pieces did little drafting and editing beyond minor grammatical and spelling corrections. Of course there is an equity question here. What of the student who did not have a significant hands-on experience with microcomputers, either at home or at school, and for whom a visit to the faculty's computer room was somewhat threatening? It may well be that as laptop computers become less expensive and more accessible we may wish to consider requiring tertiary students to be computer literate, especially using word processing, as a matter of course.

But this is an instrumental argument. More importantly, we need to consider the possibility inherent in the collaborative writing task of truth seeking. When we engage in communication that is not of a propagandist nature we aspire to 'tell it like it is'. Our aspiration is always mediated by our capacity to find the thoughts, the words, the phrases which will precisely convey what it is that we want to say. By saying it together we are making new meaning. It is true that we are never free of all of the other meaning-making which surrounds us, no text can be free of other texts, all writing then is intertextual; but collaborative writing is more transparently so, as we make our reasonings explicit to others and to ourselves.

This paper has drawn upon a range of studies which refer to the writing process and to the possibilities of the microcomputer as a writing tool. It has argued, from this intertextual base, that the principles underlying collaborative writing result in a different writing experience than when the writer works alone. In a literate society, our literature defines us. The dimensions of the definition will in the end be limited, if it is the individual voice which prevails.

References

Adams, A. and Smith, R.F. (1987) Microcomputers and collaborative talk. *Paper presented to the International Oracy Conference,* University of East Anglia.

Allsberg, C.V. (1984) *The Mysteries of Harris Burdick.* London: Anderson Press.

Barthes, R. (1975) *S/Z.* trans. Richard Miller. London: Cape.

Bigum, C., Bonser, S., Evans, P., Groundwater-Smith, S., Grundy, S., Kemmis, S., McKenzie, D., McKinnon, D., O'Connor, M., Straton, R. & Willis, S. (1987) *Coming to Terms with Computers in Schools.* Geelong: Deakin Institute for Studies in Education.

Christie, F. (1987) Genres as choice, in I. Reid (ed.), *The Place of Genre in Learning: Current Debates.* Geelong, Victoria: Typereader Publications, No.1, Centre for Studies in Literary Education, Deakin University.

Crawford, K., Groundwater-Smith, S. & Milan, M. (1989) *The Evolution of Computer Literacy and Gender.* A Report prepared for the NSW Ministry of Education. Sydney: School of Teaching & Curriculum Studies, University of Sydney.

Daiute, C. (1985) *Writing and Computers.* Massachusetts: Addison-Wesley Publishing Co.

Daiute, C. (1986) 'Do 1 and 1 make 2? Patterns of influence by collaborative authors, in *Written Communication,* 3(3), pp. 382-408.

Faigley, L. (1986) Competing theories of process: A critique and a proposal, in *College English,* 48 (6), pp. 527-542.

Groundwater-Smith, S. and Smith, R.F. (1987) *Collaborative writing & microcomputers: A question of both oracy and literacy.* Paper presented to the first joint AARE/NZARE Conference, Christchurch, NZ.

Groundwater-Smith, S. and Somekh, B. (1987) *Take a Balloon and a Piece of String. An evaluation of an electronic mail project,* Cambridge: Cambridge Institute of Education.

Kemmis, S. (1987) How schools computing is changing education, in Bigum *et al., Coming to Terms with Computers in Schools.* op cit.

Lunniss, T. (1987) The MacIntosh Project at Modbury High School, in I. Short et al., *Computers and Writing,* Adelaide: South Australian Department of Education.

Mehan, H., Miller-Souviney, B. & Riel, M.M. (1984) Knowledge of text editing and control of literacy, in *Language Arts,* 61(5), pp. 510-515.

Scardamalia, M. & Paris, P. (1985) The function of explicit discourse knowledge in the development of text representations and composing strategies, in *Cognition and Instruction*, **1** (1), pp. 1-39.

Schutz, A. (1982) *Life Forms and Meaning Structure.* Translated, introduced and annotated by H.R. Wagner. London: Routledge & Kegan Paul.

Stenhouse, L. (1983). *Authority, Education & Emancipation.* London: Heinemann Educational.

Turbill, J. (1988) Learning to write, in J. Murray and F. Smith (eds.), *Language Arts and the Learner*. Melbourne: The Macmillan Co. of Australia Ltd.

3
Multimedia, hypermedia and the teaching of English

Stephen Marcus

'What is the use of a book', thought Alice, 'without pictures or conversations?'
—*Alice's Adventures in Wonderland*

Introduction

New technologies allow words, graphics, video, film, animation, and sound to be created and combined in wonderful ways. Students and teachers are getting their hands on tools that allow them, for example, to paste their recorded voices into word processed or electronic painting documents for later playback (Bank Street Writer for the Macintosh, FullWrite Pro 1.5s, MarkUp 2.0; KidPix). They can combine real-time video with computer-generated graphics on their computer screens (Roger Wagner's HyperStudio). They can read books that 'remember' words they did not know for later review and at the push of a button, have the books 'read themselves out aloud' in different languages or rewrite themselves in different type sizes and print styles (the Discis collection). They can also, in effect, reach 'into' a film in order to tap a character on the shoulder to ask, 'Excuse me, but could you tell me a little more about yourself, and, by the way, what's that object you're holding and how does it work?' (Apple Computer Multimedia Lab).

It is difficult, writing in this essentially 'monomedia' environment, really to communicate the 'look and feel' of the kinds of tools and environments that show such great promise for transforming, not merely supplementing, students' education. I cannot really do it, of course. The most I can do is perhaps to provide static illustrations and descriptions and to draw attention to some of the 'underware' beneath the hardware and software, the educational foundations that support the technologies, that give them shape and direction.

To be sure, it is far too early to know what effects all these developments will have on us, on our students, and on our profession. Drawing on the work of Paisley & Chen (1982), we can at least frame this highly compacted question: who is learning what, from which technology, with what other effects on learning and behaviour, and, as we ask these questions, at what stage is the *development* of the technology and how advanced are we in our understanding of how to *teach* and *use* it?

Akram Midani, Dean of Fine Arts at Carnegie-Mellon University, put it this way: our involvement with new technology generally moves from an ambivalent relationship with augmented abilities to the 'dawning of irreversible change' (1986). Computer-based multimedia technologies provide students and teachers with new powers and incentives. Those individuals who have worked with these tools can provide substantial guidance, inspiration, and wisdom to help us create educational environments that support innovation, as we attempt to create educational materials that are themselves 'wonderlands', that are, in writer Joanne Koltnow's words, 'glowingly, differently alive'(see page 37).

Back to the basics: text and hypertext

Text simulates thought. Text is an artefact, representing with its own peculiar richness and its own unique limitations the ineffably complex workings of the human mind going about its business of making sense of things. Whether we are reading someone else's words or trying to represent our own intentions through writing, we are dealing with a *version* of the thought that the text represents. Text is a working-model of what we think (Marcus, 1988).

The central focus of the next few sections is not the precise degree to which text replicates our sense and sensibility. Instead, the concern is the manner in which computer technology is changing the *nature* of the product as well as the process of decoding and encoding what is on our minds. The intent is to introduce some of the basic terms, concepts, implications, and applications that provide a new set of tools, ones that enable us to construct new types of models of thought.

Videotext

To begin with, it is useful to note that the text on a computer screen (e.g. on a word processor) is neither 'print' nor 'television'(Marcus & Blau, 1983; Marcus, 1984; Marcus, 1985). Think of it as a new medium—videotext—that has its own unique messages. There are indications that this medium is intrinsically motivating, that is, adults as well as children seem to want to immerse themselves in it, to tinker or play with it (Gould, 1981; Paisley & Chen, 1982). People report that when working with a word processor, they have a heightened sense of audience for their writing (Daiute, 1983). In some strange way, the videotext itself seems sentient, akin to a kind of 'host in the machine'. In addition, many writers find that writing blocks begin to crumble as they work in a medium in which their words are not carved in stone but are written in light—they see their text ripple on a screen, disappear, reappear, or become highlighted. At the very least, when people first experience their ability to move the cursor physically through their text, they report a new sense of the 'fluidity' of their writing. (As one individual put it, 'I feel as if I'm swimming through my words!')

Neil Postman, discussing information environments in *Teaching as a Conserving Activity* (1979), notes that there are important consequences to changing the form of information, or its quantity, speed, or direction. Additionally, as Harold Innis noted in

The Bias of Communication (1964), the use of a new medium of communication over a long period of time will to some extent determine the character of knowledge that is being communicated. Individuals who are practised in creating videotext are finding that writing for television screens alters their sense of the structure of knowledge and of the language conventions used to express it (Winsbury, 1979).

What all of this means, in part, is that particularly with videotext, information does not just go into you. You go into it. You enter an environment that is shaping you even as you are shaping it.

Hypertext

Recent videotext developments are helping transform videotext and the personal computer into the interpersonal computer, encouraging and enabling collaborative reading and writing enterprises. The central construct here is 'hypertext', an information environment described in the 1960s by Ted Nelson, a Stanford University computer scientist. The hypertext notion was based on ideas articulated in the 1940s by presidential science advisor Vannaver Bush, who described the manner in which the mind 'operates by association. With one item in its grasp, it snaps instantly to the next that is suggested by the association of thoughts, in accordance with some intricate web of trails carried by the cells of the brain..[T]he intricacy of trails, the detail of mental pictures, is awe-inspiring beyond all else in nature' (1945).

Hypertext software allows individuals who are 'working at a distance to use their [electronically] linked computer screens as a shared workspace, something like a common desk. The computer capture[s] the communication, tracking and updating the information exchanged, and rendering it back precisely to all of its users' (Richman, 1987).

Here is an example of a hypertext application in a commercial setting (Richman, 1987):

> Hypertext pulls together data from disparate sources and prompts the user to check information that may bear on what he's doing. [For example], a toy company's market researcher checking a node called 'Frisbee sales' might confirm that adolescent males are the toy's biggest buyers. Searching another node called 'population trends—Minneapolis', he might discover that the city's male population aged 12 to 18 is decreasing far faster than the national average. By linking the two nodes, the researcher could conclude that his company should reduce its Frisbee distribution to the Twin Cities.

> Individual hypertext users can navigate freely among nodes, following established links. As they roam, they can add new nodes and link them to the existing network, enriching the foundation of associated ideas and creating non-linear electronic encyclopaedias (p. 132).

How in the world did we get from a presidential science advisor to questions about Frisbee distribution in the American midwest? The answer is that both concerns are at nodes in the conceptual hypertext in which the present (printed) discussion is embedded. The printed version of the 'intricate web' of associations cannot, of course, replicate the *thought*. The text can in its way model the process and product, but just as a map is not the territory, the word is not the 'think'.

A hypertext environment that may seem more congenial to the sensibilities of the present readers is the INTERMEDIA system developed at Brown University. Here, the intent was to create a means by which writers and groups of writers could 'link information together, create paths through a corpus of related material, annotate existing texts, and create notes that point readers to either bibliographic data or the body of the referenced text' (Yankelovich, 1986).

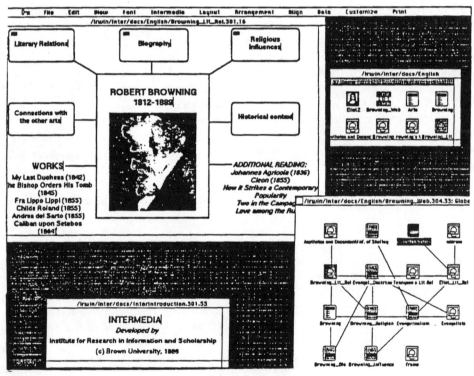

Fig. 1.

A specific application of the INTERMEDIA system, implemented in an English literature class studying the poet Browning, illustrates several important aspects of hypertext environments. Figure 1 shows a single computer screen in which a variety of 'windows' are available. Through these windows can peer the reader/writer/researcher/explorer, who can both follow and create investigative trails.

The expressed goals of the instructors for this course were as follows (Yankelovich, *et al.* 1986):

> [We] hoped that the on-line materials would help emphasise one of the implicit themes of the course—the concept that literature exists within and is influenced by a variety of cultural contexts. Our goal was to structure the material in a way which would simultaneously permit students to make a variety of comparisons between literature and other forms of art and assist them in visualising some of the enormously complex literary, political, personal, philosophical and religious influences which had helped to shape the work for each of the authors in the course. All this material, we hoped, would be presented in a fairly unstructured environment within which students could pursue their own individual interests and bring their own discoveries and insights to class discussions. Lastly, the computer could provide a means by which students could write and communicate at the same time (pp. 1-8).

This description reflects several salient hypertext characteristics. The dominant metaphor is that of an 'environment'. It exists 'on-line', that is, it is computer-based. It emphasises context and the interdependence of constituent elements, and it speaks in terms of *visually* complex patterns. It is dynamic in form and content. It is designed to be *interacted* with and depends on collaboration for its growth. It both allows and encourages the discovery of new relationships among its elements.

The INTERMEDIA system relies on a very sophisticated and unique configuration of hardware and software. A much more modest system, but one that is more generally available, is called *Guide*. This software allows the creation of videotext documents called Guidelines that contain 'buttons' (Eckhardt, 1987).

> Buttons are nothing more than pieces of text or graphics that have been given special abilities. There are three types of buttons. Replacement buttons, when clicked on, reveal new text, graphics, or other buttons. Reference buttons link the reader to other parts of the current Guideline or to other, related Guidelines. And note buttons display text or graphics that expand upon the text within the button, but only as long as the mouse button [used to 'push' the button contained in the Guideline] is depressed..

> So long as a Guideline is clearly written and logically constructed, it should be easy to navigate. Although hypertext is designed to be read on

screen, a Guideline can be converted into a [word processing] document (pp. 142ff.).

Again, we meet with some familiar metaphors. With *Guide* we 'navigate' through an information environment; the map/territory dimension is combined with the sense of fluidity. In addition, we note that the hypertext document is not designed to be printed—although portions of it can be. In contrast to INTERMEDIA, however, the links between portions of text in a Guideline are limited and set, that is, this is not a hypertext environment capable of handling unstructured investigation and discovery. Nevertheless, *Guide* serves as an example of an accessible hypertext system in which people can collaborate on the production of a 'written' document.

A related approach is taken by the software *For Comment* (Richman, 1987).

It enables a team of up to 16 members to collaborate on writing, reviewing, and editing documents that can contain up to 236 single-spaced pages. Users relay a common document they are working on—a business plan, for example—through their network of personal computers, suggesting revisions and adding up to five levels of comments and comments on comments.

The software tracks and saves each draft revision as well as all the commentators' contributions, creating a record of the ideas that influenced the group decision process. To prepare a finished document, the author simply moves suggested changes from the comment block into the main text.. (p. 132).

For Comment does not have all the capabilities of more elaborate systems like INTERMEDIA—but it does not need to. It is designed with different uses in mind. It does, however, contain a subset of hypertext dimensions in a useful and easily usable form.

Still another attempt to provide a tool for creating hypertext is *Calliope*, described as 'a tool for building a trail of ideas without having to expend effort on organising these ideas into a coherent whole until you are ready for that task'. By iconically representing and labelling (bright) ideas by light bulbs, *Calliope* allows the writer to 'capture ideas quickly as they flash into your mind, organise and reorganise [them] until they are in their optimal form, and create text files that can be further developed and edited with a word processor'. Links between ideas are made explicit by actually drawing—and redrawing—links between the idea-icons (Figure 2). Doing this automatically links the text that is created 'behind' each icon.

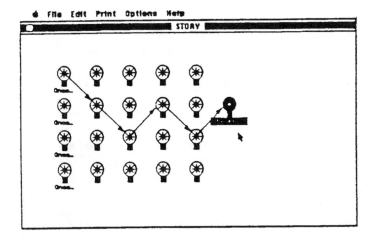

Fig. 2.

As with the other examples of software designed for use with personal computers, *Calliope* displays only a few of the attributes of a fully developed hypertext system. Nevertheless, with its emphasis on web-like representations of knowledge and its encouraging the writer to redraw the paths and patterns of meaning, *Calliope* illustrates another attempt to replicate the process and product of thought.

Interactive fiction

The hypertext construct can be applied to another related, but significantly different information environment. This is the world of interaction fiction. The discussion below merely introduces this version of hypertext in order to suggest the applicability of the concept and to broaden our perspectives on the utility of such environments.

Imagine that your computer screen describes to you the following scenario (Lehman, 1987):

> You wake up stark naked in your Manhattan hotel room. You go to the mirror expecting yourself to have blond hair, a moustache, blue eyes. Wrong on all counts: you're clean-shaven, dark, brown-eyed. The hotel accountant on the phone calls you 'Mr. Cameron', so that must be your name—though it comes as news to you. The maid at the door reminds you that you'd better put some clothes on, but there are not any in the room. It seems there is a lady who expects you to marry her in the chapel downstairs. And the police are after you for crimes you may or may not have committed. You can't remember

anything; that's your predicament. Now what are you going to do about it? Think fast (p. 67).

This fictional universe, devised by Tom Disch, is an extremely sophisticated one, both technologically and literally. There is 'not one story but many, as each move you make alters the narrative'. In addition, everything takes place in 'real time'. Events continue to unfold, time passes and situations change, even if you just sit and stare at the screen.

Less sophisticated environments have been available for some time. Often set in 'dungeons and dragons' settings, these are designed for 'readers' from elementary school age through adult. In addition, there is software that allows people to write (not just read/explore) such adventures, in which the writers create problematic situations with multiple possible evolving scenarios (e.g. *Interactive Fiction*, *Adventure Master*, *Bank Street StoryBook*, *Super Story Tree*).

Interactive adventure-writing software requires students to become 'architects of knowledge'. They are working with patterns and arrangements—mosaics of information—as they figure out how to fit all their scenes and events into the overall picture-puzzle. Student writers are establishing the information 'nodes' (i.e. the scenes and events presented to the reader). In effect, they are creating hypertext environments.

No conclusions

We know as little about electronic text as we knew about television in 1955 (Paisley & Chen, 1982). Hypertext—and hypermedia—technology is developing at a rapid rate. (Television technology, by way of contrast, has changed little over a quarter of a century.) It is really far too early to be confident about the effects of hypertext on the nature and development of reading and writing behaviour (but see Chandler & Marcus, 1985).

There is, however, a helpful framework through which we can focus our attention in order to organise and understand the developments we encounter. As noted earlier, Paisley & Chen have provided a series of questions about the effects of present and future technologies on literacy. Their overall question is this: 'who learns what from which electronic text system and with what effects on other learning and behaviour, and when does this all take place?' The last issue is of particular concern here. It deals with the temporal frame of reference of the technology under discussion. Are questions about the technology's effects on literacy being asked at the time of the students' initial or later use of the technology? And is the technology itself in its early or mature state of development?

Hypertext systems, while often sophisticated in their way, are still, relative to their potential, primitive in their conception and implementation. Extensive effort and resources are being invested in producing ever more elaborate and flexible systems, involving moving images, computer-generated graphics, and screen displays that represent information environments in three-dimensional, symbolic, and highly dynamic ways. Within this perspective, it is not unreasonable to expect that hypertext—and hypermedia—environments will have a major effect on education. An important step in this process was taken with the release of Apple Computer's *HyperCard* software.

HyperCard: what it are

The heading above is ungrammatical, but it is not nonsensical. It uses the rhetoric of error to encourage rethinking about technology and its applications. This emphasis is particularly apt in the case of *HyperCard* because it has both eluded definition and evoked a variety of literal and metaphorical descriptions. (Note: While this discussion focuses on *HyperCard*, which has had the most impact in educational settings, the comments could apply in general to similar kinds of software, like *SuperCard*, *TutorTech*, *HyperScreen*, *LinkWay*, *and Windows*.)

Figuring out how to describe *HyperCard* is not a mere exercise in semantics. It is an important part of figuring out how to revise your notions of what multimedia environments are and how they can be integrated into instruction.

So what 'are' *HyperCard*? On one level, it is a piece of software. (I mention this because many people think it is a 'card', like the kind inserted into a slot in an Apple computer.) On a metaphorical level, its creator, Bill Atkinson, describes it as a 'software erector set', meaning that it can be used to build a lot of different things. A less engineer-oriented metaphor might be that it is a loom for weaving patterns of the imagination. Both descriptions make sense because *HyperCard* involves building structures that create patterns and connections.

The 'hyper' in *HyperCard* derives from the word for 'extended', and what we are talking about here is a kind of extended index or filing card. It is one whose 'look and feel' you can design for yourself and onto which you can put text and graphics. It is also one that you can put 'buttons' on. These are simulated switches that you can push, flip, slide, or twist. Doing so will take you to other cards in a collection (called a 'stack') or move you to another stack. You can also use buttons to play sounds, operate a videodisk player or telephone connected to your computer, and do a variety of other chores, like animating your images.

So much for a basic description (which still does not do it justice). Here are some questions that attempt to get beyond the basics.

- What are useful and enriching ways to describe *HyperCard* that will reach people who have different values, cognitive styles, and ways of understanding and communicating what they know? What are some illuminating metaphors for 'knowing' *HyperCard*? (Nicol, 1987, 1988)
- What does 'interactive' really mean? What kinds of interaction can *HyperCard* supply that are the same as, and qualitatively different from, other computer-based environments? (Hooper, 1988)
- When using *HyperCard*, who exactly (including the teacher, and noting gender, socio-economic status, etc.), is learning what? With what effects on

other learning and behaviour? And when is this happening, with regard to developmental stages of the students, the teachers, and the technology (including ways of teaching it)? (Paisley & Chen, 1982)

HyperShelf

For training purposes, and to teach myself the basics of *HyperCard*, I developed a set of writing and reading activities, collectively known as *HyperShelf* (Figure 3). I shall briefly discuss some of this work below to illustrate one approach to training and curriculum development (Marcus, 1989).

Fig. 3.

- I wanted to illustrate that useful things could be developed with only a little knowledge of *HyperCard*.

- I wanted to provide teachers with some activities that could be put to use in a classroom right away.
- I wanted to illustrate the design-criteria of challenge, curiosity, control, and fantasy.

Clicking on a *HyperShelf* volume gets you to that writing/reading activity. Each volume is based on the 'Quotations' stack, a sample application that comes with the *HyperCard* program. In this stack, a quote appears on the left 'page', and the button on the right page reveals the source of the quotation. The arrows are used to move to a new set of pages. In the *HyperShelf* version (Figure 4), clicking on the small bookshelf icon returns you to the main *HyperShelf* 'menu'. (There is also a hidden button that allows students to add their own comments on the quote.) Additional pages with new quotes can easily be added.

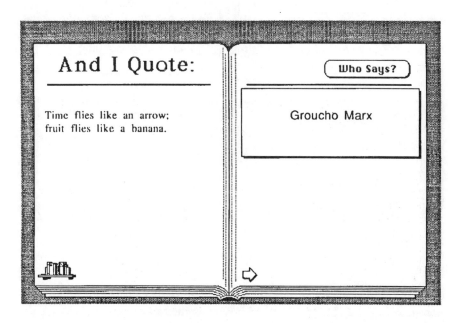

Fig. 4.

Two other examples will suggest how this basic structure can be easily modified merely by cutting and pasting buttons and text fields (which transfers their capabilities) and by modifying the way they look.

In 'Mathimagine' (Figure 5) each set of pages contains five different kinds of writing prompts, based on the calculator-type buttons. The scrolling text field on the left-hand page can contain the equivalent of about eight typewritten pages. 'Mathimagine' currently has eight sets of pages, or 40 writing assignments. (*HyperShelf* as a whole contains about 300 writing prompts.)

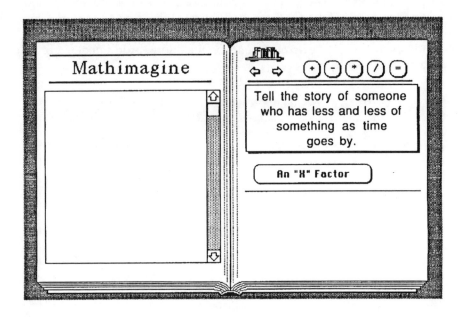

Fig. 5.

In 'Aesop' (Figure 6) the students can read colonial American versions of Aesop fables, which rather than being 'dumbed down' as they often are in textbook versions, are reproduced with the vagaries of spelling and pronunciation retained, along with illustrations drawn from the same sources. The text requires more active and challenging engagement than might otherwise be the case. Students can add their own comments about the fables, and *Hypercard's* search feature allows them to find topics or comments of particular interest to them. Additional fables can of course be added.

Again, *HyperShelf* was designed to provide a variety of writing and reading activities, all based on one model. The intent was to show how quickly you can use *HyperCard* to develop material for classes. There are very extensive *HyperCard* applications available, but we can also make our own. One of the beauties of the tool is how many tools it is -- and how adaptable to our needs. (Perhaps another way to describe it is as the Swiss Army Knife of educational software.) While *HyperShelf* is in many regards a very simple application of a very powerful programming environment, it has served to illustrate to teachers many of the facets of *HyperCard* that are at their disposal.

Fig. 6.

HyperFiction

HyperCard has also inspired a genre of courseware sometimes marketed as 'hyperfiction'. The usual comparison is to choose-your-own-adventure stories like those mentioned above, in which the reader determines the particular course of events by the choices he or she makes at various points in the reading of the story. *HyperCard* has allowed the addition of multiple links, animation, and sound to what has traditionally been predominantly a linear, print medium.

With *HyperCard*'s object-oriented interface, you usually make your choices by pointing at something on the screen (e.g. a door) and clicking the mouse button to 'open' it in order to explore what lies beyond. The example below, from Amanda Goodenough's *Inigo Stories*, illustrates the general approach (Figure 7).

Fig. 7.

At one extreme, in terms of certain kinds of complexity (and number of screen buttons), are products like Amanda Goodenough's *Inigo* and *My Favorite Camel* stories, which are visually sparse but which are exceptionally charming and have a particularly endearing quality. At the other extreme are environments like *The Manhole* and *A Country Christmas*, both of which are highly complex and visually lush.

All these stacks are good examples of intrinsically motivating computer environments, containing as they do elements of challenge, curiosity, control, and fantasy.

These stacks can also be seen as interactive visual databases. Future applications will undoubtedly make use of *HyperCard*'s capacity for making pictured scenes (e.g. a room filled with objects) serve as an interface for storing and evoking personal knowledge, using memory-aid systems like the ones developed by the Greeks and medieval scholars.

Commercially available stacks like *The Manhole* and the *Inigo* series were not designed as instructional environments. Generally speaking, the journey is its own reward. (However, a stack like *A Country Christmas* does have instructional, or at least informational, dimensions in its design, e.g. having a globe serve as the interface for getting information about Christmas customs around the world.)

Classroom applications

Until such curriculum-specific applications *are* widely available, it is possible to generate educational activities as collateral material for existing stacks. The examples below illustrate how *The Manhole* could be used in a variety of ways in a language arts class. None of the suggestions is fully developed—or necessarily could be. As listed here they are designed, as a group, merely to suggest a range of possibilities.

The activities could be done individually or in groups. No grade level is indicated although some activities are clearly more demanding than others.

- Students would go on a Scavenger Hunt, using a list prepared by the teacher or by previous classes of students who have had a chance to explore the program. Student groups would have a set amount of time to 'bring back' information contained in the 'world' presented in the stack. The more playful and puzzle-like the list is, the better. Examples: Find a rabbit's advice. Bring back the sound of a walrus's voice.

- Students would draw maps of the trips they took below the manhole, adding their own comments about what they found.

- Students in groups or individually would be asked to make a list of as many objects as they could find that began with a given letter of the alphabet. This assignment could be modified to have them find as many sounds as they could that began with a specific letter.

- Students would write stories based on the trips they took. A class anthology could be put together containing the stories, as well as students' own illustrations.

- Students would develop a guidebook for future travellers, containing tips and directions for how to get the most out of their trip. (The group would have to decide first what 'most' meant.)

- Students would develop a clear set of directions for telling someone how to get to a certain place in *The Manhole's* world. Other students would try to follow the directions without making mistakes.

- Students would write a description of one 'scene' in the stack, with enough detail so that people who had never used the program would recognise it once they got there.

- Students would make a list of things they wish would have happened during their trips through the world, but did not. They could develop stories based on these alternative events.

- Students could start with a given scene, describe it, and then write a story based on their own imaginations, i.e. without using any of the events that have been designed into the stack.

- Specialised Scavenger Hunts could be designed (see above). Students could be asked to find as many sounds as they could in the stack, or as many smells as they imagine might go along with the pictures (e.g. the smell of cedar in a chest of drawers).

- Students would be asked to focus on a particular scene and list as many objects as they could that appeared in that scene. (Correct spelling might or might not count, depending on grade level.)

The sample activities above assume the stacks are not themselves being modified to incorporate reading and writing features. However, one of the wonderful features of *HyperCard*-like environments is that teachers and students can relatively easily make simple modifications that allow students to revise the images on the screen. They might also add their own words to the pictures in the story by typing them into text fields that have been added to the images. This is usually one of the first tasks language arts teachers set for themselves when they are first trying out their skills at using *HyperCard*.

HyperCard and hypermedia

Teachers are quick to sense the excitement and value of hypermedia environments, for example, using *HyperCard* to control a laser-disc player or to play back students' voices that have been 'pasted' into their stacks. Those who have been involved in such hypermedia educational environments have been at the forefront of discovering that what *HyperCard* 'is' is defined by what's done with it. The sections below deal with the general issue of innovation and with some of the 'savvy' regarding *HyperCard* that has developed in the course of its use in the classroom and in teacher training.

'If it works, it's obsolete'

This is an awkward fact of life in the world of computers, as expressed by Alfred Bork at the University of California, Irvine. By the time the bugs have been found and fixed, by the time the potential of the basic tool has been realised, the next generation of hardware or software has often superseded the original vision upon which the earlier product was based.

When it comes to working with *HyperCard*, I think it is important to remember one of the key questions posed above: *at what stage in the development of the students, teachers, and the technology itself are we asking our questions?* Much of the current expertise in implementing *HyperCard* in the schools is being acquired precisely because the tools and methods *are* in their formative stages. Everything does not work yet. We do not yet know *how* best to get things to work. As will be suggested below, however, this is a perfectly acceptable state of affairs when it comes to fostering innovation.

Interviews and metaviews

Writer and educational consultant Joanne Koltnow has conducted extensive interviews with people around the country who are exploring *HyperCard*'s potential in the schools. She was very gracious in allowing me to interview her about her interviews. In so doing, I was fortunate to be able to gather quite a few perspectives on how people are defining *HyperCard* by what they do with it.

The items noted below are based on conversations with her and a review of published material describing people and projects (Apple Computer, 1990). While the portions in boldface should be credited to Koltnow, she is not responsible for my annotations (although she certainly contributed to them), nor should any particular comment (hers or mine) be attributed to any specific teacher, site, or project.

If a student uses *HyperCard* to make a flashcard stack, it is more okay than if a teacher does the same thing. In either case, this amounts to filling a new medium with an old content and hardly takes advantage of *HyperCard*'s special qualities. Still, it is important to have the student practising decisions about what's worth knowing and developing the problem-solving and computer skills necessary to implement the student's own ideas.

Beware of situations in which a student-teacher's 'collaboration' consists of a student's doing the scanning and typing for a teacher's great stack idea. While there is something to be said for students learning new technological skills (e.g. how to operate a flatbed scanner or a video camera/digitise), it does a disservice to their education and trivialises the term 'collaboration' to limit their activity this way.

A stack might be a great resource for students, but the person who had the most fun and learned the most was probably the person who created it. This is not to say that, for example, a world geography stack is not valuable, but to call it interactive may again be misrepresenting an important notion. It is worthwhile asking ourselves if the personal excitement and satisfaction that come from working with *HyperCard* are not best shared by giving students themselves the tools rather than a finished product.

Are the teachers and students who are doing great things with *HyperCard* the same ones who were doing great things before, or does *HyperCard* allow an even wider population to benefit from its special advantages? Institutions achieve excellence by 'drawing on the potential of the average person to achieve extraordinary results' (Peters & Waterman,

1983). It would be a shame if *HyperCard* became another tool for the technological elite in a school. If so, neither *HyperCard* nor personal potential is being realised, and perhaps the patterns of training and support need to be reconsidered.

You do not have to teach kids to think non-linearly. Teachers are more able now to encourage and see the value of 'getting off the track'. With *HyperCard*, it is more true than ever that the journey can be the reward. This may mean that we'll have to emphasise in different ways the value of staying *on* the track, but it is nice to have a tool that is suited to right-brained, association-based thinking, a style of making sense and meaning that has its own particular strengths and richness.

HyperCard **lets kids participate according to modality strengths.** We have long recognised the value of trying to reach students through a variety of sense modalities. *HyperCard*, along with sound and image digitisers, provides us with some powerful multimedia tools. Just as importantly, we can put these powerful tools into the hands (eyes, and ears) of our students.

Do not underestimate what your kids can do; or the age level at which kids can do things. In the early days of word processing, some elementary teachers were teaching their students *WordStar*, a program that has daunted many adults. Watching a two-year-old using *MacPaint* (including opening and closing documents) can perhaps prepare us for Seymour Papert's assertion that computers will allow children to write before they are able to talk. We would do well to consider carefully what kids can teach us about what *HyperCard* is and what they can do with it.

'Nothing never happens'

There is, of course, no single prescription for successful or exceptional innovation. In point of fact, the bit of wisdom introducing this section (provided by high school teacher Aaron Hillman) serves to remind us that we should value what may seem to be false starts, wrong turns, and poorly implemented paths and plans. We are all in the early stages of understanding what *HyperCard* is and what we can do with it. We need to pay a special kind of careful attention to our own and others' experience as we explore what *HyperCard* can do for us and to us. And we would do well to follow the advice given to those who aspire to excellence in innovation: 'Make sure you make a reasonable number of mistakes' (Peters & Waterman, 1983).

I have noted before that *HyperCard* provides students and teachers with new powers and incentives. The experiences of *HyperCard* pioneers provide substantial guidance and inspiration for a wide variety of informal 'rules', along with both wild and educated guesses. We should combine this collective wisdom with what we know about encouraging environments that support innovation.

Concluding remarks

If, as suggested above, text simulates thought, then hypermedia environments go several steps further in representing, in Vannevar Bush's words, 'as we may think'. Hypermedia tools, in fact can be understood as allowing us to build models of our thought processes as well as the content of our thought. This is what Havholm & Stewart (1990) suggest in their discussion of how to actively involve students 'in apprehending how ideas and information connect'. Their students studied two theoretical texts: the Russian formalist Vladimir Propp's *Morphology of the Folktale* and Aristotle's *Poetics*. The general goal was for the students, using two hypertext software systems, to build 'working models' of the two literary theories, models that could be used actually to produce the kinds of texts that the two theories purported to describe.

On the basis of the class's experience, the instructors concluded that

> [T]he operation of literary theory (and, by extension, the operation of many theories in the humanities and social sciences) can be modelled or simulated. Hypertexts in *Guide* did simulate the operation of intertextuality, and *HyperCard* programs did model some aspects of the production of narratives according to the theories of Propp and Aristotle....[No matter how] crude or partial the models, their examination as a kind of deductive 'result' of the theory made it possible for students to be unusually clear about the powers and limitations of the theories themselves. (p. 48)

To consciously mix metaphors and media, I might suggest, also, that hypermedia documents may give voice to a variety of equally valid mental maps. Hypermedia may thus provide a crucial set of tools to provide to writing students, if, as several sources have proposed, there may be significant—equally valid and effective—rhetorics that are characteristic of different cultures and genders.

George Gadda (1991), for example, drawing on the work of Kaplan (1966), has discussed the 'predictable differences between paragraphs written in English by students with...various first languages; to describe these differences Kaplan wrote that "superficially, the movement of the various paragraphs...may be graphically represented" ' as follows (Figure 8):

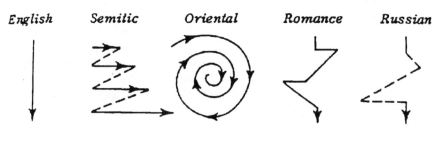

English   Semitic   Oriental   Romance   Russian

Fig. 8.

Kaplan characterises the development of paragraphs written by Arabic students, for example, as 'based on a complex series of parallel constructions, both positive and negative'. Asian writing, on the other hand, is 'marked by what may be called an approach by indirection, [showing] the subject from a variety of tangential views, but...never looked at directly' (Kaplan, 1966).

What is intriguing here is the manner in which Kaplan's and Gadda's discussions evoke the notions of alternative paths through a body of knowledge. In the context of hypermedia, what is often called the architectures of knowledge and cognitive processes may give rise to very different rhetorical architectures. Likewise, discussion of gender-related issues in the teaching of writing makes a case for broadening instructional goals. An examination of these issues has clear analogs to those of Kaplan and Gadda.

Some argue that such cultural and gender-based issues amount to a kind of special pleading that has little to do with the appropriate demands of writing instruction, except as a way to categorise what's 'wrong' with certain students' efforts. The point here, however, is not to enter that particular fray. It is merely to suggest that such concerns, considered in the context of hypermedia environments, enrich rather than confuse the issues. They provide thought provoking perspectives from which to understand the often immediate and compelling attraction of a collection of technologies, tools that often combine and contrive to help us get the most out of our students and the most out of ourselves.

References

Apple Computer (1990) Macintosh K-12 Success Stories Guide (MO847LL/A); Learning How to Write Means Learning How to Think (MO391LL/A), and Inspiring Educators: True Stories About Macintosh in Schools (MO802LL/A). Cupertino, CA: Apple Computer, Inc.

Chandler, D. & Marcus, S. (eds.) (1985). *Computers and Literacy*. Milton Keynes: Open University Press.

Daiute, C. (1983) The Computer as Stylus and Audience. *College Composition and Communication*, 34(2) pp.134-45.

Eckhardt, R. C. (1987) Glimpsing the Future With Guide, in *MacWorld*, (February), pp.142-45.

Gadda, G. (1991) Writing and Language Socialisation Across Cultures, in *With Different Eyes: Insights into Teaching Language Minority Students Across the Disciplines*. Los Angeles, CA: University of California pp. 55-74.

Gould, J. (1981) Composing Letters With Computer-based Text Editors, *Human Factors*, (23) pp. 593-606.

Havholm, P. & Stewart, L. (1990). Modelling the Theory of Operation. *Academic Computing*, March, pp. 8ff.

Hooper, K. (1987) *Summary: Multimedia in Education*. Cupertino, CA: Apple Computer, Inc.

Innis, H. (1964) *The Bias of Communication*. Toronto, Canada: University of Toronto Press.

Kaplan, R. B. (1966) Cultural Thought Patterns in Intercultural Education. *Language Learning*, (16), pp. 1-20.

Lehman, D. (1987) You Are What You Read, *Newsweek*, (12), January, p. 67.

Marcus, S. (1984) Real-Time Gadgets With Feedback, in *The Computer in Composition Instruction*. William Wresch (ed.), Urbana, Illinois: National Council of Teachers of English, pp. 120-130.

Marcus, S. (1985) The Host in the Machine: Decorum in Machines Who Speak. *IEEE Transactions on Professional Communication*, PC-28,(2), pp.29-33.

Marcus, S. (1988) Reading, Writing, and Hypertext, *College Literature*, Vol. XV, No. 1, pp. 9-18.

Marcus, S. (1989) What Are HyperCard? (Parts 1-4). *The Writing Notebook*, Sept. 1989 through May 1990.

Marcus, S. & Blau, S. (1983). Not Seeing is Relieving: Invisible Writing With Computers. *Educational Technology*, (April) pp. 12-15.

Midani, A. (1986) A Matter of Perception, Featured address, *EDUCOM '86*, Pittsburgh, Pennsylvania.

Nicol, A. (1987, 1988) Children Using HyperCard. *Working Paper Drafts, Human Interface Group.*, Apple Computer, Inc., Cupertino, CA.

Paisley, W. & Chen, M. (1982) Children and Electronic Text. *A Report for the National Institute of Education, Institute for Communication Research*. Palo Alto, CA: Stanford University.

Postman, N.(1979) *Teaching as a Conserving Activity*. New York: Delacorte Press.

Richman, L. R. (1987) Software Catches the Team Spirit. *Fortune*, 8 June, pp.125ff.

Winsbury, R. (1979) *The Electronic Bookstall*. London: International Institute of Communications.

Yankelovich, N. (1986) INTERMEDIA: A System for Linking Multimedia Documents. *IRIS*, Brown University, 5 September, pp.1-15.

Yankelovich, N. Landow, G.P. & Cody, D. (1986) Creating Hypermedia Materials for English Literature Students. *IRIS*, Brown University, 8 October, pp.1-8.

Additional resources

Ambron, S. & Hooper, K. (eds.) (1987) Learning Tomorrow, *The Journal of the Apple Education Advisory Council*, Spring 1987.

Ambron, S. & Hooper, K. (1990) *Learning with Interactive Multimedia*. Redmond, Washington: Microsoft Press.

Apple Computer, Inc. (1989) *HyperCard Stack Design Guidelines*. Wokingham, England: Addison-Wesley.

Bush, V. (1945) As We May Think, in *The Atlantic Monthly*. A shortened version appears in Conversational Computers, pp. 10-12, William D. Orr (ed.), New York: John Wiley & Sons, Inc., 1968.

Fraase, M. (1990) *Macintosh Hypermedia: Uses and Implementations (Volume II)*. London: Scott, Foresman.

Kaplan, R. B. (1988) Contrastive Rhetoric and Second Language Learning: Notes Toward a Theory of Contrastive Rhetoric, in Purves A.C.(ed.), *Writing Across Languages and Cultures: Issues in Contrastive Rhetoric*. Beverly Hills, CA: Sage Publications.

Malone, T. (1981) Toward a Theory of Intrinsically Motivating Instruction. *Cognitive Science*, (4).

Nielsen, J. (1990) *Hypertext & Hypermedia*. London: Academic Press.

Peters T. J. & Waterman, R. H. Jr. (1983) *In Search of Excellence*.

Seyer, P. (1991) *Understanding Hypertext* Blueridge Summit, Pennsylvania: Windcrest/McGraw-Hill.

Tognazzini, B. (1992) *Tog on Interface*. Wokingham, England: Addison-Wesley.

Software mentioned and related products

Adventure Master, CBS Software, One Fawcett Place, Greenwich, CT 06836

Bank Street StoryBook, Mindscape, Inc., 3444 Dundee Rd., Northbrook, IL 60062

Bank Street Writer for the Macintosh, Scholastic, Inc., 730 Broadway, New York, NY 10003

Calliope, Innovision, P.O. Box 1317, Los Altos, CA 94023

A Country Christmas, B & B Soundworks, P.O. Box 7828, San Jose, CA 95150

Culture 1.0, Cultural Resources, Inc., 7 Little Falls Way, Scotch Plains, NJ 07076

Discis, Discus Knowledge Research, Inc., 45 Sheppard Avenue East, Suite 410, Toronto, Ontario, Canada M2N 5W9

For Comment, Broderbund Software, 17 Paul Drive, San Rafael, CA 94003

FullWrite Pro 1.5s, Ashton-Tate Corp., 20101 Hamilton Avenue, Torrance, CA 90509

Guide, OWL International, Inc., 14218 NE 21st St., Bellevue, WA 98007

HyperScreen, Scholastic, Inc., 730 Broadway, New York, NY 10003

HyperShelf, Intellimation, Dept. Y4KJ, 130 Cremona Drive, Santa Barbara, CA 93116

HyperStudio, Roger Wagner Publ., 1050 Pioneer Way, Suite P., El Cajon, CA 92020

Inigo Gets Out,, The Amanda Stories and *Your Favorite Camel*, The Voyager Company, 2139 Manning Avenue, Los Angeles, CA 90025

Interactive Fiction, Eastgate Systems, 138 Brighton Ave., #206, Boston, MA 02238

KidPix, Broderbund Software, 17 Paul Drive, San Rafael, CA 94003

LinkWay, IBM Educational Systems, US Marketing & Services, Dept. ZVO, 1133 Westchester Avenue, White Plains, NY 10604

The Manhole, Mediagenic, P.O. Box 3048, Menlo Park, CA 94025

MarkUp 2.0., Mainstay 5311-B Derry Avenue, Agoura Hills, CA 91301

MindMap, William K. Bradford Publishing Co., 310 School Street, Acton, MA 01720

Super StoryTree, Scholastic, Inc., 730 Broadway, New York, NY 10003

SuperCard, Silicon Beach, 9770 Carroll Center Rd., Suite J, San Diego, CA 92126

TutorTech, Techware Corp., P.O. Box 151085, Altamont Springs, FL 32715-1085

4
Beyond the metaphor: breakdown and realignment

Jon Pratt

Metaphors are risky. At their best, when they are on our side, they help us to clarify and conceptualise our environment and make sense of its operations. As teachers and educationalists, we use metaphors a lot; children, in particular, learn by comparison.

But metaphors can turn. Fifth columnists in our midst, what is intended to clarify and illuminate may only serve to obscure and obfuscate. Metaphors lead us into unfamiliar territory and, like fickle guides, leave us there. But I must be careful; I am becoming metaphorical.

Computer programs use metaphors. We are asked to use pens and palettes, to cut and paste, to create pages, files and folders; this is the metaphorical language of computer interfaces and operating systems. The electronic obscurity is rendered meaningful by metaphorical reference to a world of familiar human operations we understand.

Magpie, an excellent and innovative program for the Archimedes computer, is introduced in the manual with these words:

> *Magpie* is an application which allows you to create 'ring binders' of pages.
> The pages appear in sections, between dividers, as in a real ring binder.

It is surely sensible that we should make this metaphorical appeal to reality; only in this way can we enmesh the power of new technologies with our understanding of tasks which confront us.

Yet I recall being taken to task by an astute Advisory Teacher for Information Technology after I had spent some time introducing databases to a group of children by drawing a comparison with card-filing systems.

> 'What makes you think that their range of experiences makes them any more familiar with card indexes than computers?' he asked.

I had no answer.

> 'In any case why refer to an inferior technology at all? Why not offer them the database as a source of information to explore?'

Pedagogy is inter-related with curriculum in such a way that changes in pedagogy inevitably change the curriculum; indeed changes in pedagogy are a necessary, although usually not a sufficient, condition for any planned curriculum change.

The use of computers cannot merely change the way in which learning takes place but may also change significantly the way we think about and understand learning. However, Eraut (1988) examined claims that computers would achieve some transformation of the learning process with the conclusion that 'the insertion of a computer rarely affects either the curriculum or normal classroom practice: its use is assimilated to existing pedagogic assumptions'. The Parliamentary Office of Science and Technology reported that some (teachers) use technology to deliver the same curriculum as it existed before; others use it to create a whole new curriculum. Again, Somekh & Davies (1991) offer a more radical and expansive view:

> The development of a pedagogy for IT is the process whereby we learn to interrelate creatively with computers in educational events. The machine becomes an expression of human endeavour and growth: its opportunities are exploited; it is not in control. Yet it is more than a tool since it embodies in one form or another a capacity to interact with us as a surrogate of its human programmers.

The capacity for transformation

How, therefore, may teachers be brought to an understanding of this capacity for transformation, the development of a new pedagogy? This chapter draws on the experiences of teacher-researchers in the PALM Project[1] to show how their exploration of ideas of child autonomy using computers brought them to complex questions and ideas about the culture that computers generated in their classrooms and the implications for children's language development. PALM chose the techniques and principles of action research on the assumption offered by Stenhouse (1975) that:

> It is the teacher who, in the end, will change the world of the school by understanding it.

---

(1) PALM (Pupils as Autonomous Learners Using Microcomputers) was a two-year research project funded by the National Council of Educational Technology in association with Cambridgeshire, Essex and Norfolk LEAs and based at CARE, the University of East Anglia, UK. It was led by a central team of co-ordinator (Bridget Somekh), three project officers (Jon Pratt, Bob Davison and Erica Brown) and a secretary (Laura Tickner). PALM was directed by John Elliott and joined during the second year by Richard Davies.

Teacher researchers in PALM were, therefore, invited to research and develop the use of computers within their classrooms and schools in the light of their own professional experience and beliefs. The Project Officers supported the teacher researchers by offering information gathering and analysis techniques. The emphasis was not on authoritarian ideas of 'teacher improvement' but on the idea of collaborative reflection, discovery and understanding.

It was a route that brought them to positions like this conclusion by Jean Edwards in 'I Like to Read' (PALM Publications • Teachers' Voice 16, 1991).

Jean Edwards had spent two years researching the relationship between the use of adventure games and story writing programs such as 'Desktop Stories' with her 7-8-year-old Pakistani children:

> Despite all this has autonomy taken place? Are there signs of autonomy developing? What has happened to these children during this period?
> They have entered a tunnel warily - at the narrow end, traversing the pitfalls and treasures and emerged into the daylight, larger, stronger, wiser and far more confident, ready to enter a new tunnel with eagerness and anticipation . . .
>
> . . . The autonomy lies in the developing relationship between the children using the computer as a catalyst. The activities created an atmosphere in an insular, escapist world where divisions have to be made, creating a sub-culture where different rules apply and control is available over the ultimate goal and the paths to it.

Although these concluding paragraphs may be guilty of some hyperbole, I find the imagery and metaphor arresting. The concept of transformation implicit in Jean Edwards' words and choice of metaphor go beyond the simplicity of change in learning processes caused by the substitution of the computer for other resources or 'tools'. The suggestion here is that the transformation of the pedagogic culture is both difficult and, indeed, painful with different lessons to be learned not only for children but, crucially for teachers themselves. It is perhaps no surprise that teachers found writing about their experiences not merely a 'reporting task' but an extension of their own transformational understanding. Significantly, their words echo the experiences they identified in their pupils.

Jaqueline Illsley from South Greenhoe Middle School, Swaffham,UK, sees writing as:

A kind of catharsis which allows the writer to give substance to what is happening in the classroom . . an opportunity to crystallise thoughts and ideas, to have a starting point from which one can progress.

As Almas Baker of Gladstone Primary School, Peterborough UK, wrote:

> I've always found writing difficult but I thought since I'd only be describing what's gone on in my classroom, it won't be quite so bad, but - painstaking, laborious, excruciating and more were all words I'd use to

describe my efforts. . .

And, yet, writing has been the most valuable part - it has helped bring ideas and thoughts into sharp focus and helped crystallise all those other half-thoughts and ideas lurking in the background.

Breakdown and realignment

Vince Moon, a teacher of Year 6 children at Longthorpe Primary School, Peterborough, UK, observed how children working on computers ignored the normal practice of clearing and tidying up five minutes before the end of a school session, a process which all children normally carried out automatically out of habit. The children's behaviour, Vince Moon concluded, was not wilful in the sense of a rebuttal of authority nor was it simple forgetfulness; they were operating in a different, an alternative culture.

More significantly, perhaps, Vince Moon saw a reflection of this process in his careful research into the children's learning during extensive computer-based Newsday simulations. The children were well used to group work, but with the introduction of computers, Vince Moon observed immediate changes in group behaviours:

> The children tried to impose some order on their discussions. Tentatively, they put up their hands to speak as though they were unsure whether the usual class 'rules' still applied. At this point I wondered if I had asked too much of the children. Imposed organisational strategies would have solved these 'problems'.

Vince Moon recalls how 'normally' the children would have made grateful requests for him to act as arbiter in disputes or difficulties, a situation he may also have imposed upon them. On this occasion, however:

> . . this organisational 'improvement' would have been at the expense of the individual pupil's autonomy. Some pupils certainly did appreciate the importance of the freedom they were given during the day. One girl, Joanne, summed this up nicely in her comments after the day: 'Mr. Moon could have (at the beginning) said: 'You can do this' and 'You can do that', but we wouldn't have had any say in it and it wouldn't really have been our work.'

As Vince Moon's research progressed through a number of cycles in which he repeated and modified the work with different children, he was concerned to deal with important practical issues concerning timing, pupil grouping, suitability of resources, distribution of computers and so on. But increasingly, he found himself able to create a deeper understanding of the learning culture that was being created and his role within it:

As progress towards developing autonomous learning situations occurs, the role of the teacher radically changes. For the teacher, order and clarity of task are valuable, maybe essential, aspects of classroom management. Yet for pupils to develop their own autonomous structures for learning (using computers) a period of breakdown and realignment may be necessary.

The disappearing teacher: culture shifts in the classroom

This understanding of shifts and changes both in the teacher's role and in the pedagogic culture of the classroom has echoes in the work of other teacher researchers. Barry Williams from the Ailwyn School, Ramsey, Cambridgeshire, UK, undertook a project with a Year 9 History class in which they were given open access to a range of software including word-processors, databases and a hypertext program, *Genesis*, in a term's work on a local History research topic. Pupils were largely responsible for managing their own learning of the programs and for selecting the software appropriate to their needs.

Again, although the students were accustomed to group work and to historical research topics, the use of Information Technology in this way was a new experience for both teacher and pupils. Barry Williams decided to approach his research in this way:

> I felt it was important to record two 'versions' of this 'story' - my own perceptions and ideas of what was happening and those of the students. To this end I invited six students to become co-researchers. I asked them to keep their own PALM diaries while I kept mine so that we could share our thoughts on the project.

It became evident that significant shifts were taking place as the work progressed. Barry Williams observed:

> The previous pupil/teacher relationship which was the usual one of expert teaching and guiding the not so expert has not functioned. . . . . In fact many of the pupils rapidly overtook me in their understanding of the computer and its capabilities.
> Any teacher embarking on this type of work will find his/her relationship with students subtly change. The old idea of resident expert will disappear to be replaced with that of provider, facilitator and, sometimes, organiser. Even the last is beginning to disappear.

What became apparent to Barry Williams and others was that these changes were not simply due to possible lack of teacher expertise; they were rooted in the ways in which children and computers interacted and in critical differences that computers brought to the nature of student learning experiences.

John McGowan from Arthur Mellows Village College carried out detailed research into children's use of Art programs:

> What is different . . is that all the processes are carried out within an enclosed environment. Whereas, in the making of a print or a ceramic piece there are various halts and checks built into the system, which allow the teacher to monitor development, by constructing projects that are wholly contained within the machine there are no natural breaks in the activity, no reason for the pupil to bring that work into contact with others.

Barry Williams, also realised the implicit risks in the learning culture he had produced. He recalls how pupils 'rarely called upon me to help perhaps realising they had outgrown me in this particular field' but expresses concern that some students 'became accustomed to working independently and did not ask for help' in situations where they needed guidance and support. In order to ensure that he was able to share the students' language with them and to offer critical support and guidance, Barry Williams had to evolve different, more flexible, strategies of intervention.

It is not surprising that many teachers felt considerable tension between their accustomed role as the guides of children's learning and the different types of learning culture which computers invited. In many cases teachers felt a strong sense of responsibility for 'structuring' children's learning with computers, sensitive to the vulnerability some learners may feel if they engage with resources beyond their mastery.

The disappearing computer: the focus of research

As the work of the PALM project progressed and an increasing number of teacher researchers were starting their explorations, those of us with responsibility for guiding the project were also experiencing complementary tensions. The project had as a central purpose the testing of the hypothesis that there was a direct link between the use of computers and the development of pupil autonomy.

However, in much of our teachers' work the focus seemed much broader, concerning itself with larger questions concerning how teachers organise and participate in children's learning. Certainly, this exploration was instigated by the introduction of computers into their classroom work but where was the detailed examination of the direct interaction between child and computer? We termed this anxiety 'The Disappearing Computer'.

There is of course a potential dilemma in any large-scale action research project which has central objectives. If teachers, correctly, are encouraged to see their research as something for which they have ownership and control and which exists fundamentally for the purposes of their own development, then how can a coherent focus and theory be achieved from potentially disparate sources?

In an attempt to resolve this issue, the first PALM conference at the end of the first year brought together 40 teacher researchers and invited them, by sharing their experiences, to draw up a number of common themes and issues. These in turn were formulated into questions to be used as an analytical basis for subsequent work.

1   It has been suggested that autonomous learning consists in some combination of these characteristics among others: choice; confidence; responsibility for one's own learning; creativity. How can these be encouraged and how can the computer help?

2. Is structure necessary to autonomous learning? If so, what kind of structures in classrooms lead to autonomous learning?

3. Can individuals within groups be autonomous? If so, what kinds of group work with computers are effective in leading to autonomous learning?

4. What differences in the teacher's role are brought about by the use of computers in the classroom? How and when should teachers intervene in the learning process?

5. Is autonomy in learning a similar process for all? Or is it specifically related to age, ability, gender or culture?

6. What kinds of context/environment support autonomous learning? If there are aspects of the classroom or school which act as constraints can these be changed and can computers help?

It was clear to us that the opportunity to reflect upon the introduction of computers into their own pedagogies, coupled with the capacity action–research methods offered to perceive the normally unseen or guessed at, was leading the PALM teacher researchers towards a broad critique of their classrooms as learning environments and cultures.

Rather than being a deflection from the central focus of computers as an aid to autonomous learning, this was an essential and prerequisite process of discovery.

Soon after the first conference I made an attempt to construct a model of the ideas of child autonomy in the classroom environment that our teacher researchers were offering. I wanted to try and trace the interconnections between quite disparate experiences. From their notes and early writing, it appeared that there were a number of dimensions of autonomy which meshed in dynamic interaction in the classroom. In some respects, these dimensions serve to reflect that the school is inherently an anti-autonomous institution in that, to a greater or lesser extent, it seeks to structure, co-ordinate and predict the learning behaviour of the individual.

The model (Figure 1) does not seek to be an accurate representation of actual behaviours but a way of enabling teachers to reflect upon their role in the culture of their classrooms. If the four dimensions were key components of the fabric of learning experiences for pupils, then the extent to which pupils had control and mastery of them was a reflection of their qualified autonomy as learners. Clearly, on this basis, autonomy could only be achieved by a balanced development across all four dimensions of experience. Inevitably, however, such development would be unbalanced and dependent on a number of factors like the level of maturity of individual pupils.

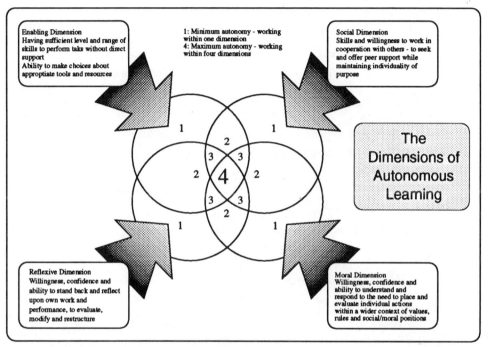

Fig. 1.

Part of the role of the skilled practitioner was judging the degree of compensatory support required within one or more dimensions of pupils' experience.

However, it would be easy for teachers to over-compensate, to over-teach within one dimension and by so doing deny development for their pupils. In the complexity of the classroom environment, with its multitude of interactions and events, its culture, this would usually be obscured. Tabberer (1987) remarked that: '(there is) a problem of over-teaching ... a tendency for teachers to overcome pupil difficulties by failing to set them'.

It is here that the introduction of the computer into the classroom can effect such change by bringing significant changes to pupil experiences within a dimension. Thus the computer can enable pupils in important new ways while at the same time demanding new patterns of collaborative working which test the social dimension of autonomous learning. So the computer has the potential to act as catalyst for significant changes in the normal pedagogic patterns of classroom life.

It appeared to me that this was what was happening in the classrooms of PALM teacher researchers, most of whom had little or no experience of the use of computers in the classroom. This was the 'breakdown and realignment' described by Vince Moon. To understand precisely how computers developed children's learning, this broader pattern of change had to be explored and understood first.

This was clearly moving away from Papert's (1980) view of the capacity of computers to follow a Piagetian model of development in which children become 'builders of their own intellectual structures' and develop the freedom to learn 'without being taught'. There was greater empathy with Kutnick's view (1990) that children develop from 'an egocentric domination into a sociocentric world':

> Realisation that others may have a different point of view from oneself and the ability to adjust to this moves the child into a 'social-centric' world. Thus, knowledge is seen as a social process resulting from actions with others; development is not just simple discovery by the child, it is a discourse between the child and others.

Shared perceptions

It was this developing understanding that allowed teacher-researchers to share and reveal commonality in quite diverse experiences.

Gail Guest from Longthorpe Primary School, Peterborough, UK, describes how she introduced concept keyboards into emergent writing strategies for four-year-old children:

> . . To begin with, the children needed to experience a play stage with the concept keyboard and I attempted to introduce a more structured activity far too quickly. Playing with the computer and keyboard and printer provided fascination for all and, as with play in all areas, the children were absorbing knowledge across a wide area of the curriculum. Their understanding gained through playing with the computer only really began to make itself apparent at a later stage.

It is interesting that the importance of play in the development of children's learning with computers surfaced in teachers' reflection and planning in more unexpected areas.

Claire Brookes of Ernulf Community School, St Neots, Cambridgeshire, UK, records early attempts to teach the use of word processor and database programs to Year 8 students through a highly structured approach. This had led to disappointment in terms of their expectations that children would interrogate a database (about the disparities in wealth and life expectancies between 'first' and 'third' world countries) to form their own views and opinions as a preparation for further writing tasks.

. . it became apparent that many children were unable or reluctant to interrogate the database to explore ideas or hypotheses of their own. One boy, when interviewed, commented:

'I would have preferred to have had loads of books and looked it up in books'.

When asked to explain this view, he said:

'Because I would learn more because the computer was doing it for you'.

To this student the computer appears to **substitute** for learning rather than to enrich or to enable it - reduced to the role of a simple tool.

Claire Brookes realised that, in an attempt to clarify and help students through anticipated difficulties, she had suppressed a vital part of the learning culture which computers invite and demand:

. . the students were left to 'play', to experiment with the computers and find out for themselves what they could do. Groups reported back to others and taught them and us what they had discovered.

Of course, all PALM teachers felt it necessary to re-evaluate their roles carefully in order to strike a workable balance between their responsibilities towards students' learning and the potentially conflicting demands of child autonomy.

Dawn Fuller of Brampton Junior School, Cambridgeshire, UK, explored this dilemma in detailed research into ten-year-old-children's language development while using the *Typesetter* desktop publishing program:

I felt more able (after a first run through with the program) to devolve, replicate and refine my learning experiences for the children and to begin to provide a learning experience which was more meaningful and independent, in which children were free to take risks and develop their own strengths.

For there always exists in any classroom that fine balance between learning new things alongside and with the children, and putting them in a situation where frustration sets in.

Careful thought needs to be given by the teacher to making (the program) accessible and allowing the children to discover the program's structure and potential for themselves.

Teacher rejection: the threat of the machine

We should not underestimate the potential and real stresses for teachers in this situation. Denise North, an English teacher from St Helena School, Colchester, UK, expresses her own fears with great honesty and eloquence in her research journal:

At a personal level I feel that the dynamic control of the lesson might be dissipated by the machine. . . I suppose that the idea of children being hunched over machines with just their backs facing me is a kind of rejection of me as the main resource in the classroom. E. M. Forster pointed out that human beings need 'to connect' with each other on various planes: intellectual, emotional, spiritual and physical. This contact seems to me to be under threat when people become obsessed with machines.

We as teachers, feel pressurised into competing with the 'hi-tech' world that children live in outside school.

Autonomy engendered and facilitated by the computer can also place children in positions of stress and difficulty where it runs into conflict with established values and practices.

Joan Evans of Springwood High School, Kings Lynn, UK, tells the story of Steven whom she describes as an 'oddity' and an 'outsider' whose language skills were erratic. Steven, along with other children, was given a laptop computer to use for work in school. While other children succumbed to some of the practical difficulties of using the computers, Steven seemed to use his regularly and with enthusiasm.

However, it became apparent that there was conflict in lessons. Teachers complained that Steven was using the computer to be disruptive and that he was pursuing his own writing rather than the tasks set. They found it difficult to pin this down when his work was 'in the computer'.

Joan discovered that Steven was producing a whole range of writing of his own including a 'confession' of his feelings to the computer, left on the computer disc and a revelation to his teachers. Joan comments:

> The point behind all this was that Steven was retreating more and more into a fantasy world of his own. He was using the computer to aid him in this.
>
> How far was he capable of doing this without a computer? Would he have reached such a stage without the computer. I think not. I feel that the machine opened up new horizons for him and showed him the possibilities for escaping his environment. It could be the wish to escape was always there but the computer gave strength and realisation to those wishes.
>
> I reached an annoying sort of paradox. While I felt that Steven was gaining some important skills and a new depth of knowledge in several directions, I also felt the frustrations of other members of staff that Steven would not conform.

The ideal of change

If, therefore, teachers are to be equipped for continuing developments which lead to ever more powerful technology, then their needs go beyond personal mastery of the technology and an understanding, however valuable, of how it relates to the whole curriculum. They will need to understand how the introduction of computers may challenge, question and realign the pedagogic culture of their classrooms and how they can modify and adjust their own roles as teachers in the light of these changes.

We must go beyond the available metaphors which seek to define the experience offered to the teacher and learner by computers and recognise that there is the power available to enable us to think differently; a liberation is possible. But 'breakdown and realignment' are continuous processes inherent in the dynamic of change which develops a healthy society.

Dewey in 1961 offered this vision:

> Particularly it is true that a society which not only changes but has the ideal of such change as will improve it, will have different standards and methods of education from one which aims simply at the perpetuation of its own customs.

For many PALM teachers, this learning process lead them into areas of professional knowledge and reflection which almost caught them by surprise. Marlies Marshall wrote this as a conclusion to her research with seven and eight-year-old Pakistani children at Gladstone School, Peterborough, UK, completed just before her retirement:

> How does autonomy of pupils affect the teacher? I am not ready to answer this, but I know what happened during our research in working with the microcomputer. I became a pupil with my pupils, we no longer stood apart. We were experimenting, we were sharing our experiences and we were brought together by a common interest. My role had changed to a friend, an adviser, an interested party - who at this stage could only make suggestions, comments, and give encouragement - but no answers.
>
> The children saw that even teachers have to learn - and that teachers too can make mistakes before they learn. This changed the atmosphere in class. The change of emphasis from pupil/teacher relationship to that of a team radiated into all areas of the curriculum. The children showed more interest, I felt myself becoming more accessible. Our relationship became more open and trusting, it was more relaxed and our mutual respect was growing.
>
> The children came with their discoveries, they posed their problems. We were able to discuss these and even to arrive at some answers. At this stage I began to feel that teaching is much more than providing knowledge, it can also be a rich and satisfying experience for both children and teachers. Perhaps autonomy in learning will ultimately lead to a form of de-schooling changing the whole system of education in a dramatic way.

References

Dewey, J. (1961) The Democratic Conception in Education, Chapter 7, in *Democracy and Education*. Macmillan, New York.

Eraut, M. (1991) *The Information Society - A Challenge for Educational Policies? Policy Options and Implementation Strategies*. Cassell, London.

Kutnick, P. (1990) Social Development of the Child and the Promotion of Autonomy in the Classroom, in Rogers, C. & Kutnick, P. (eds.) *The Social Psychology of the Primary School*. Routledge, London.

PALM (1990) *The Teachers' Voices* series:
- **Baker, A.** *Computers and Language Enhancement with Bilingual Children*
- **Brooks, C. The** *Developing World - Children and Data Handling*
- **Edwards, J.** *Computers and Children's Reading*
- **Evans, J.** *PALM at Springwood High School: Special Needs Department*
- **Fuller, D.** *The Pursuit of Excellence - Children and Desktop Publishing*
- **Guest, G.** *Hannah is Writing a Lot! Computers, Autonomy and Reception Children*
- **McGowan, J.** *From Lascaux to Archimedes - introducing Artisan into an Art Curriculum for Year 9 Pupils*
- **Marshall, M.** *'Image' and Child Autonomy*
- **Moon, V.** *Making the News*
- **North, D.** *Unpublished Paper*
- **Williams, B. The** *Bury Project*

Available from CARE, University of East Anglia, Norwich NR4 7TJ

Papert, S. (1980) *Mindstorms: Children, Computers and Powerful Ideas*, Harvester Press, London.

Somekh, B. & Davies, R. (1991) Towards a Pedagogy for Information Technology, *The Curriculum Journal* , 2 (2) pp. 153-170.

Stenhouse, L. (1975) *An Introduction to Curriculum Research and Development*, Heinneman Education, London.

Tabberer, R. (1987) *Study and Information Skills in Schools* NFER Nelson, London.

5
Computers and the writing process: a memo to the Head

Chris Breese

Dear Mr Shakespeare,

As you are aware I have been running a project in the school for the last three years which has given children unlimited access to word processors in order to study the effects upon their writing. I hope to use my conclusions, recorded here, as the basis for discussion at the next meeting of the Curriculum Committee.

The potential benefits of using word processors in the teaching and learning of writing skills are well documented both anecdotally and in the academic papers of a small army of researchers. We were lucky enough to attract the necessary support of The Advisory Unit for Microtechnology in Education, based in Hertfordshire, UK, to set up an experiment to investigate what the benefits might be in the context of a working classroom.

Each child in one class was given a laptop computer to use and take home 'as personal property' and all the writing done in English lessons was done using the word-processing program built into the machine. The class was a mixed-ability group of 23 children chosen at random from our first-year intake. The range of ability was very wide, varying from children whose writing showed a fair measure of technical control through to very weak users of language. The group did not have any **really** accomplished young writers.

The children used the computers to write in English lessons and I collected all their written efforts in order to compare how their work changed draft by draft and also over a period of time. The control group was another class from the same year using pen and paper methods.

Perhaps the most obvious change is the apparent increase in motivation observed when children use word processors for writing. This has been recorded by several researchers and our project bears out this phenomenon. Certainly the children talked with much animation about what they were doing. There was a lively and positive atmosphere in the classroom which centred around their discussion of their work and that of their friends. Moreover, after examining the texts produced when the children were writing narrative and comparing them with written narrative produced by a parallel class in the same year it became clear that the test children wrote on average 30% more than their counterparts using pen and paper. This, in itself, is quite exciting especially as it tends to be true not only of children whose work is already enthusiastic but also of those who have been reluctant to write at length before.

This increased motivation shows two distinct features - more time is spent 'on task' and longer pieces of writing are produced. These are distinct because the longer pieces are possibly a temporary effect associated with novelty and reluctant writers often relapse into their unenthusiastic ways after a period of time, while the extra time spent appears to be a long-term effect of children learning to redraft, observing its benefits in their own writing and continuing to redraft their work as a matter of common practice. Even the reluctant writers appear more likely to redraft their work once they have seen the benefits. They may be writing less than they were in the first flush of enthusiasm but they are more careful with what they do write. Without word processors easing the chore this would surely be less likely to take place.

The 'care' that writers show is twofold - 'getting it down' (composing and developing the ideas) and 'getting it right' (editing). The composition and development part of the process is important in that it allows for the thinking through and the incubation of ideas. During this process the writer often sets new goals and sees different possibilities for the development of a piece of writing, while selecting appropriate language registers from experience. For inexperienced writers the teacher's support as a language consultant is often essential during this phase as a source of language models and advice on organisation and clarity. This part of the process can be, and often is, time-consuming but the benefits can be enormous. In an attempt to create a vigorous language environment, the children were seated in groups and encouraged to talk about each other's work and exchange ideas - standard practice in most English classes throughout the country. I was centrally involved, as the teacher, in discussions with the children about the qualities of their drafts and tried to place suggestions or options rather than be specific and directive. This appears to be the time during which ideas are turned over, improved, expanded or rejected. A great deal of language-intensive work goes on as children see possibilities and hatch new ideas. Frequently they even see new horizons and the original text becomes dramatically altered as a result as though the idea has incubated. It is during this period in the writing process that the teacher's input can be most effective because the child writer is making decisions which are, at first, too complex to be undertaken without guidance. Gradually, as the child acquires 'a critical eye', the teacher can move away and encourage independence.

The editing process is the final step the writer takes, during which the grammatical elements of the written texts can be checked. I have already suggested that if the first intervention by the teacher is at, or after, this stage a great opportunity is missed for helping the child to clarify not only her thoughts but also her means of expressing them in writing. It is essential that this difference between drafting and editing is understood clearly because teachers, and, therefore, the curriculum itself, need to be sensitive to the time requirements of the whole writing process. Writing will not be well served by time constraints.

In the following extracts one of the project children, K, has tried to write about finding a giant on a beach. K was a 13-year-old boy of moderate ability and something of an under-achiever. We had studied photographs of a huge fibreglass man lying on an Irish beach in readiness for the filming of *Gulliver's Travels* and we had discussed the possibilities for a piece of writing.

Draft 1

I was walking along the beach the cool fresh air blew in my face the sea washed over my feet and birds where singing and in the distance I could see a little fishing boat. kkkkkhhh ooooooohhhhh! kkkkkkhhhhhooooohhhhh what was that noi.. AGHHHH a giant hand. I ran all the way to the town and when I got there I told the mayor. The mayor immediately called out the soldiers they ran onto the beach and tied the giant down with hundreds of ropes. When he woke up he tried to move but he could not. He struggled and struggled he snaped one of the ropes.

K's first draft is a short effort of approximately 110 words. It starts brightly enough:

'...the cool fresh air blew in my face the sea washed over my feet and the birds where singing and in the distance I could see a little fishing boat.'

This pictures a certain idyll and appropriate images are used to express it. There is a touch of cliché but the 'distant fishing boat' is unexpected and vivid - a touch of originality. Alas this is unsustained and the rest of the story hurries along to its unsatisfactory ending via the discovery of the giant, the return to town, the action of the mayor and his forces and the struggle for freedom of the giant. In achieving this brevity K has not added any detail to give the picture some life other than the noises 'kkkkkhhh ooooooohhhhh!' and so on which denote the giant on the beach. The piece ends abruptly as though K has lost interest. In short it is a disappointing piece of writing.

Draft 2

I was walking along the beach the cool fresh air blew in my face the sea washed over my feet and birds where singing and in the distance I could see a little fishing boat. kkkkkhhh ooooooohhhhh! kkkkkkhhhhhooooohhhhh what was that noi.. AGHHHH a giant hand. I ran all the way to the town and when I got there I told the mayor. The mayor immediately called out the soldiers they ran onto the beach and tied the giant down with hundreds of ropes. When he woke up he tried to move but he could not. He struggled and struggled he snaped one of the ropes. Half of the soldiers ran for it. But I wasn't scared. He looked at me I stared at him. We both stared at each other I suppose he was asstonished by my size like I was asstonished by his size. He struggled again and sat up I did not budge he reached out for me I let him pick me up.

Between the two drafts the class had discussed the development of ideas with me. We talked about the difference size might make to the smell, to the sounds made (breathing etc.) and how figurative language might serve a purpose in bringing these ideas to life. I was not prescriptive.

K has responded, not by taking on the suggestions, but by making an interesting development of the idea of relative size:

'...I suppose he was asstonished by my size like I was asstonished by his size'.

He does not sustain this effort and again ends the story abruptly - indeed at the very moment when an interesting development could have taken place. He has seen the need for development, has made a decision as to where and what, but there is no real evidence of discrimination at work or close involvement with the story. He seemed to have no real notion of what to do or change and the potential of the text remained unfulfilled at this stage.

Draft 3

One morning I was walking along the beach. The sunrise shone across the sea. The seagulls were flying in the sky, there was a little fishing boat out at sea. There was a palm tree directly in front of me on the mound. The cool fresh air was blowing my hair back. My lively Doberman was running across the warm golden sand the sea tide was splashing across my feet. Then a coconut fell off the tree and cracked on a stone, my dog Toby ran up to the coconut and licked up the milk. There was a dead fish on the beach with a seagull ripping its insides out, it made me feel sick. It smelt disgusting. I saw my dog run over a sand dune, so I ran over it as well. "What the ef" was that it's so bit it's gianormous i,i,i,i,t's a giant footprint. Look there's more of them". I followed them. They went on for miles Toby ran on again so I whistled to him to come back but he didn't come back. I walked around the corner, it was only then that I realised the beach was empty, a sudden chill ran down my back. Ah he'd found an old piece of leather that was buried in the sand. He was tugging and pulling like a shire horse with a cart. I helped him pull, it must have weighed a ton. After a while and a lot of energy I pulled it out it was a giant shoe. A cold air blew around my body. I looked at my watch it was 7.30. I looked around where was Toby, I saw his tail wagging above a little sand dune. I ran over to the dune I thought he had found a bone or something. My heart was still in my throat because of the shoe. I ran over to the dune where I looked for my dog. He was looking down a well or something where has he gone. He just flew up into the air. Wow I was moving Ahhgg. Ugh. Where was Toby there he was he had hurt his paw. "There's that giant let's get him". Lucky I'm a cop I pulled my Colts out of my Bermudas and started shooting at the giant, my bullets where all hitting him in the head. He fell to the floor, my magazine ran out, I picked up a piece of wood and started hitting him. Then suddenly my partner Joe gave me a machine gun I wondered where he had come from but I started shooting the giant again. I walked home with my dog and my partner leaving the giant laying dead on the beach. When I got home I ran myself a lovely hot bath. After that I never touched a gun again. I was fired from the police I didn't know why but now me and my dog - Toby's son, Toby died about a year ago. Now I've got my own business called GIANT-BUSTERS. I've made a lot of money and bought myself a Ferrari Testarossa and a Suzuki.

This draft, Mr Shakespeare, was submitted a week after the others. K had simply allowed the idea to sit in his head for a time until a more satisfactory story emerged. This version has a completeness about it lacking in the others. The beach scene is vivid with original thinking and even the Doberman is 'lively'. As we move closer to the giant - he doesn't just appear this time - there is a growing sense of fear:

'...a sudden chill ran down my back.'

'...a cold air blew around my body'.

The story structure does not degenerate this time. K works towards an ending in which he lives happily with Toby's son in a world characterised by symbols of success. It is true that this symbolism is familiar enough to be dubbed 'derivative' in a mature writer, but in one so young (13 years old) it is more a matter of the writer reaching for symbols he recognises from his own limited experience (TV, books and middle-class aspirations in general). It is a much improved piece of writing, as I am sure you will agree, Headteacher. (Incidentally, he has not yet edited the text, in case you are wondering about his grammar...).

The point I wish to raise at the Curriculum Committee meeting is what this piece of writing tells us. I am sure you would agree that the first draft would usually be the only draft because time puts pressure on teachers who need to cover a syllabus or a body of knowledge and this is especially true of subjects other than English. K would be labelled as a poor writer and his language weaknesses would be highlighted as only a part of the problem. He apparently lacks imagination. The evidence of a first draft alone is damning. The second draft, produced within minutes of the first, is merely an extension of the first, displaying very little improvement and would do nothing to change our minds. The third draft, however, shows K in a very different light - a writer of imagination and much skill in shaping a narrative to build suspense and, finally, to satisfy the reader with a neat ending. He is a much better writer than the first draft suggests. This phenomenon, akin to incubation, is common when children are allowed time to dwell on their writing and are given the means to alter the text dramatically without effort.

So, Mr Shakespeare, we have a dilemma. The use of word processors motivates children to spend more time and care over their writing by removing the chore of rewriting. The redrafting process and the associated period of incubation often enhances the writer's perception and understanding of the writing task and therefore helps to improve the finished product. Do you remember *The Bullock Report - A Language for Life*? It set us all thinking about the breadth of activities associated with the learning of language and is as important today as it was in 1975. It stated quite clearly 'children learn as certainly by talking and writing as by listening and reading'. This is true right across the curriculum - yet how often do we allow time for that process of learning-through-writing to take place? The experience provided by this experiment suggests that children become more actively involved in discussing their work when involved in writing **as a process** and benefit accordingly. The word processor makes the process of writing much less arduous than it is using pen and paper or a typewriter and the children find it easier to become involved as a result. When writing is simply a unidirectional business with no time allowed for revision or redrafting then the children are deprived of the chance to review their work and do not make the same progress. It is that simple.

Laid against that there is the pressure of the scale of the whole curriculum. Already we have staff complaining, with some justification, about how they are under pressure to finish a crowded syllabus in the time allotted. How can it be possible for the school to take advantage of what the word processor offers?

My proposals are the following:

1. The school should discuss a writing across the curriculum policy as soon as possible. This should establish the process of writing as at least as important as the product, in order to allow the children to learn through writing. It is essential that a coherent approach to writing is established throughout the school. The children should be given the security of knowing that their writing will be nurtured by the same principles no matter what the context in which the writing takes place.

   To this end a series of in-service training sessions should be organised with a view to raising awareness of approaches to the development of writing and its role in learning across the curriculum.

2. As it is established that children benefit from using computers for their writing and that they lose the acquired benefits if the computer support is withdrawn, the school should investigate how it can provide maximum access to computers for all its children. This would possibly necessitate reviewing the timetabling priorities and establishing a strategy for the expansion of computer facilities within the school. If providing unlimited access by giving each child a computer is considered

too expensive then we should investigate how closely we can approximate to this ideal circumstance within the frame of our own budget. The ideal mix would be a number of laptop computers (to service children's needs when they wish to take work home, for example) and a substantial network system within the school to allow access whenever children need to write formally, at least.

The use of the computers should be opened out to each subject area in which writing plays a part. Rooms will need to be equipped with printers (at least two in each room) and staff will need to be trained in the use of the equipment. Only by taking this step can we expect to develop coherent approaches to writing across the curriculum.

3. We know that a process-centred approach to writing is time-consuming and therefore problematic for some teachers with crowded syllabuses. Therefore the curriculum should be 'mapped' and, using that evidence we should initiate an appraisal of cross-curricular approaches. For example it is clear that as language specialists the English department could play a more active role in the writing requirements of other departments, supporting, for instance, the writing of a report on a Geography field trip or the description of an experiment in the Science lab. The whole curriculum could then be delivered with less duplication and, I hope, more effectively.

At the end of the day, Headteacher, it is important that our experience with computers as writing tools is not merely an interesting, but transient, phase in the history of the school.

This project has suggested how appropriate use of computer technology can transform language development given a rational and informed approach to the process of writing - and how this, in turn, improves the quality of learning. All of this is made much easier by using the computer but is unattainable unless we build our learning and language development practice upon these foundations. No amount of computer equipment will compensate for poor curriculum design and ill-informed practice.

I look forward to our discussions at the next meeting of the Curriculum Committee.

Chris Breese

6
What is important in writing? Some differences in attitude between word-processing and handwriting pupils

Mike Peacock and Bahman Najarian

Introduction

This paper presents evidence that - despite a paucity of experimental research findings detecting an improvement in the quality of word-processed pupil writing - some experienced pupil users of word processors are beginning to show clear signs of attitudinal change in the ways they conceive of writing. The study examines the attitudes of six classes of first and second-year secondary school pupils (groups which either were or were not experienced word-processor users) to three aspects of writing: the surface (or secretarial) features, the 'meaning' (or compositional) features, and the task constraints imposed on their writing[1]. The word processor users have each had their own Z88 'laptop' machine since September 1988[2].

The dearth of research findings detecting consistent short-term measurable improvements in the written work of pupils using word processors is clear from the pages of *Dissertation Abstracts International*. A broadly similar pattern looks also to be true of revision; there are very few examples of consistent evidence of an increase in the number - or quality - of revisions to their writing made by pupils using word processing technology (for example: Duling, 1985; Fulton, 1988; Haas, 1987; Hawisher, 1986; Morrow, 1989; and many others). Despite this, an abundance of anecdotal and press evidence suggests that people involved in using word processors to assist pupil writers frequently become convinced that there has been an improvement in the quality of the work. Much of this perceived improvement is difficult to substantiate: many fall victim to simplistic technological determinism (Finnegan, 1988); qualitative accounts frequently blatantly ignore massive additional teacher assistance in their accounts of the supposed benefits of word processing (Peacock, 1990); controls are seldom used; the effect of print itself on the perception of assessors may be discounted (Peacock, 1988).

However, despite the absence of a clear pattern to the experimental evidence, and the many doubts surrounding anecdotal accounts, it is difficult to deny that the environment provided by a word processor is very different from that provided by pen and paper. Furthermore, a recent qualitative study based on a series of informal interviews with experienced pupil users of word processors seemed to hint at attitudinal changes - particularly in the way writing was approached - when they were word processing rather than handwriting (Peacock & Breese, 1990). In particular, some of the pupils seemed relatively unconcerned about 'getting it right' when word processing:

Sasha: I just write away. And if you make any mistakes you can just delete them away.

Andrew: I just write. I type what I think and then after that if you have ideas what you do is just fill it in - with block movements or just filling in.

Helen: I plan it a bit differently cos you can't really be scruffy on paper otherwise you have to scrub it all out and do it again and you don't want to.

Jason: (Using pen and paper) you have to be more prepared. You have to make sure you don't make mistakes. And it wouldn't really matter on the computer and I wouldn't really bother.

Comments such as this seemed to indicate an attitude to writing that was not dominated by issues of correctness. The main concern is to get ideas down first (and tidy up the 'surface' features later, if necessary). If this is so, and experienced student word processor users do indeed tend to become less concerned about the secretarial (or surface) features of writing, does this mean that they are likely to become more concerned with the compositional (or 'meaning') features of their work - that is, with the **quality** of what they are writing? Certainly this is the assumption underpinning many anecdotal accounts. The different medium offered by this new writing technology is frequently assumed by enthusiasts to hold out the promise of beneficial improvements:

It seems that freedom from the chore of copying out emancipates young minds (Sawford, 1989).

To phrase it more formally, it seems likely that the ability to treat successive drafts of one's writing as only an approximation to what one is really trying to say is intimately bound up with potential for development as a writer. As Stein (1986) puts it:

The important feature of the review process is that writers can treat their texts as a piece of discourse to be understood... They can attempt to make sense of their own writing (p. 229).

Then, assuming the validity of the Faigley & Witte (1981) findings (see Note 1) - that 'expert' writers make more compositional revisions than progressively less-skilled writers - and coupling this with the evidence of attitudinal changes to surface revision by the young users of word processors, an important possibility arises. If their attitude to surface revision alters, are these young word-processing writers beginning to develop an attitude to writing characteristic of 'expert' writers? Even if so, of course, there is no guarantee that the pupils will become better writers. However, it seems reasonable to argue that pupils who develop a functioning awareness of the value of the compositional aspects of writing, have available a cognitive tool that is not available to pupil writers whose conception of writing (and/or revision) is more restricted.

Methodology

This paper is perhaps best seen as the more specifically focused part of a two-part study; the other part being based almost entirely on a series of informal interviews with experienced pupil word-processor users (Peacock & Breese, 1990).

Evidence was sought from both handwriting pupils and experienced word-processor users about their attitudes to surface, compositional, and contextual features of writing. Comparison is made between attitudes of pupils at a southern school and at two northern schools nearly 200 miles away, and across two year groups. The three-fold aim is to examine whether experienced pupil users of word-processors display signs of any difference in attitude to the surface, the compositional, or the contextual features of their writing relative to their handwriting contemporaries.

A three-section questionnaire was developed, piloted, and presented to a total of 135 pupils from six different classes and from two different year groups at three different secondary comprehensive schools - one in Hertfordshire (School H1) and two in Yorkshire (Schools Y1 and Y2). The pupils were all in mixed ability classes (Table 1). The questionnaire was identical for all classes, and was presented to all by the same person using the same explanatory outline. The Year One classes were tested in June, 1989, and the Year Two classes almost exactly one year later in June, 1990. The 'Z88 user' class was tested twice. The four non-user classes were all independent of one another, although the Year Two (south) classes ran parallel to the Z88 users at the same school, and were from the same range of feeder primaries and the same catchment area. All the schools were mixed comprehensives with pupils from age 11 through to age 18, although the southern school is rather smaller than the two northern ones. Additionally, care was taken to use classes that had teachers with very different teaching styles (see Note 3).

TABLE 1: Group size and distribution.

	W/P users	W/P non-users	
Year 1	Group A (School H1) n=18	Group B (School Y1) n=29	Group C (School Y2) n=23
Year 2	Group A (School H1) n=18	Group D (School H1) n=15	Group E (School H1) n=18

Section A of the questionnaire consisted simply of two open questions: 'What are the most important things to do when attempting (1) to write a good story, and (2) to improve the story'. The pupils were asked to spend up to three minutes jotting down any aspects of their writing that they considered relevant to (1) and then (2). This section was designed to settle the pupils down, to focus their thoughts on writing, and to pick up aspects of revision that might fall outside the areas covered in Section B.

Section B was the key section for the purposes of this paper and consisted of 18 randomly presented questions, to be answered with a mark on a five-point scale. The questions consisted of five questions about writing behaviour relating to the major categories discussed earlier - 'surface', 'meaning', and 'context'. There were also three questions aimed at minimising the chance of pupils answering in erratic or random fashion, perhaps because they did not understand what was being asked of them. Eight papers were excluded on these grounds, leaving a data sample of 127 pupils. After having the rubric explained aloud to them, the pupils were given up to five minutes to work through the 18 simple questions. All the pupils were, of course, unaware of the general sub-divisions underlying the particular questions (for details, see Note 4 and the Appendix).

Results

Results are presented in sections corresponding to sections A and B (significance level <0.05). (Section C was a catch-all asking if the pupils had any further comments. It was there to keep particularly speedy finishers of Section B busy, if necessary. The comments elicited were few, and have not been included in the analysis.)

Section A

A total of 30 randomly selected section A replies from each group (users and non-users) were categorised into 143 surface, meaning, or contextual comments. No comments fell outside these categories although occasional mention was made of aspects not covered by the questionnaire. For example, two of the pupils mention the noise level in the classroom (classified as contextual) as a factor affecting their writing.

The results lend broad support to the more detailed interpretations made in the light of the section B results.

The findings are:

1.   That the users consistently mention surface features less frequently than the non-users (18.2 per cent as against 27.3 per cent).

2.   That users make slightly less mention of 'meaning' features than non-users (24.5 per cent as against 26.6 per cent).

3.   That 'contextual' features are very seldom mentioned at all by any of the groups (3.5 per cent in total).

Section B

An analysis (Mann-Whitney) of attitudes to the three aspects of writing, controlling for the different **year-groups** of the children, found no significant differences between the handwriting groups relative to one another (Surface: <0.66; Meaning: <0.24; Context: <0.23), or between the word processing group tested near the end of the first year and near the end of the second year (Surface: <0.36; Meaning: <0.62; Context: <0.39) (see Note 5).

TABLE 2: Word processor users compared to non-users (Mann-Whitney U):

| | Mean Ranks | | | | |
	Users ($n=36$)	Non-users ($n=85$)	U	Z	Corrected 2-tail prob.
Surface	33.13	72.81	526.5	-5.7	<0.00
Meaning	48.90	66.12	1094.5	-2.5	<0.01
Context	56.26	63.01	1359.5	-0.9	<0.33

When all the word processor users and all the handwriters were compared, however (Mann-Whitney), very significant differences became apparent (see Table 2). Chi-square analysis based on low, medium, and high categories of awareness produced very similar findings (see Table 3).

TABLE 3: Word processor users compared to non-users using chi-square analysis (responses grouped into three categories: low importance (5-11), medium importance (12-18), and high importance (19-25)):

	Chi-sq.	df	Prob.	
Surface:	24.43	1	<0.00	(Users score lower)
Meaning:	5.87	1	<0.02	(Users score lower)
Context:	0.49	1	<0.48	

Surface features: The null hypothesis (that word processor users and handwriters would not differ in their attitudes to 'surface' features) was **not** confirmed. All the individual items in this category (punctuation, spelling, paragraphing, use of capital letters, and neatness) were rated as of significantly less concern to the word processor users than to the handwriting pupils.

Compositional features: The null hypothesis (that word processor users and handwriters would not differ in their attitudes to compositional features) was **not** confirmed. Four of the individual items (trying the story out on others, frequent revision, finding exactly the right words, and working out a story-line) had lower means (less important) for the word processor users than the other pupils, but not significantly so. The category 'Keeping the reader interested' was rated significantly less important by the word processor users.

Context: The null hypothesis (that word processor users and handwriters would not differ in their attitudes to 'contextual' features) was confirmed. There were no significant differences on any measures in this category (all fell around the 0.3 or 0.4 mark). (However, the two factors in this category to be rated as slightly more important by word processor users related to time and length. When talking to the users, comments were frequently made about these two things: about how much longer it took to produce most things on the machines as against handwriting them, and about the ease of counting the exact length of a story - to the word - because of the machine's built-in word count facility.)

Discussion

What is causing what? The absence of any significant differences between handwriting pupils - be they at northern schools or southern, or in the first or second year, or in relatively large or small classes, or at a large or small school, and with four different class teachers involved - strongly suggests that it is indeed prolonged use of the word processor that is the variable largely responsible for the dramatic change in attitude to the secretarial aspects of writing of the experienced word processor users.

Secretarial v. Compositional features: This finding that the experienced word processor users do indeed tend to attach **less** importance to the surface features than do the handwriting groups is not very surprising. Some such change has been widely predicted and can convincingly be argued to be readily understandable as the pupils' response to the facility of the word processor not to penalise mistakes by necessitating rewriting of text. A tentative justification might go something like this: 'It is easy to correct spelling mistakes and punctuation and things, so I can forget about all that and just concentrate on the story.'

Attitudes to 'meaning' changes: What may be surprising, however, is that these experienced word processor users do **not** seem to 'just concentrate on the story' - the compositional features of writing - more than their non-word processing counterparts. Indeed, the evidence suggests that the pupil word processor users also attach less importance to the compositional features of their writing than the handwriters. Since four of the five section B 'meaning' categories were not individually significantly different between the word processing groups and the handwriters, it is probably sensible not to make too much of this, but it certainly seems safe enough to argue that there are no signs whatever of word processor users beginning to take the compositional aspects of their writing more seriously than handwriters.

Attitudes to context: The very few references to contextual features in the less structured Section A suggests that, taken as a whole, these task constraints are of much less concern to all pupils than both surface features and 'meaning' features. This finding is probably masked by the equal number of questions about context, meaning, and surface features in Section B.

Conclusion

Rather than ask why pupils are not moving towards taking composition more seriously - given such a clear alteration in their attitude to secretarial features - it might be more sensible to ask why so many teachers of writing have expected and predicted such a move. Reasoning analogously, if children are given an increase in their pocket money, do we seriously expect them to begin to use the extra cash to buy something good for themselves instead of an extra fistful of sweets? To expect pupil writers (or anyone) to do what is good for them just because it is possible, is a little naive. Powerful technology - like increased spending power - confers **choice**, not a pre-determined course of action. The additional freedom is dependent on all sorts of other factors, such as teacher direction, peer group pressure, and parental attitudes to schooling, to name but three obvious ones.

To generalise, then, it would seem that as pupils become experienced in the use of word processors they do indeed quickly adjust to the obvious features of the machine which make writing less onerous. They do not, however, respond anything like so readily to the possibility of support offered by the word processor to those prepared to make greater cognitive efforts. All the evidence points to the tendency of pupils to develop more nonchalant attitudes to writing when using word processors. Pessimistically, this means that even when pupils acquire the technologically-assisted potential to improve, they frequently fail to utilise it effectively. Optimistically, however, they are clearly capable of change.

Bring on the teachers.

Notes

1. The first two features are particularly familiar. For instance, in the recent English National Curriculum document, *English for ages 5 to 16* (DES, 1989), a distinction is made between 'the composing aspects of writing and the secretarial aspects' (17.1), with the recommendation that:

    > The main principle is that the secretarial aspect should not be allowed to predominate in the assessment while the more complex aspects of composition are ignored.

    A similar distinction has been made by Faigley & Witte (1981). Working entirely with handwriters, they propose a 'taxonomy for analysing revision':

    > Which is based on **whether new information is brought to the text or whether old information is removed in such a way that it cannot be recovered through drawing inference.** We call changes that do not bring new information to a text or remove old information **Surface Changes.**

    Changes that do result in the addition, deletion, or alteration of content are called **'Meaning Changes'.** (pp. 401 and 402.) Faigley and Witte found that a group of six 'expert adult' writers (journalists and published writers), six 'advanced' writers ('from an elective, upper-division expository writing class'), and six 'inexperienced' writers ('deficient in writing skills') differed widely in the percentage of 'meaning changes' they made to a piece of writing. 'Meaning changes' accounted for 34 per cent of the revisions made by the experts, for 24 per cent of the changes made by the better students, but only for 12 per cent of the changes made by the least able writers.

2. The computer used was the Z88 'laptop'. The whole thing is no bulkier than a telephone directory and a lot lighter at two to three pounds. It has a full-size keyboard and a built-in six-line screen. 'Resident' software includes a word processor called *Pipedream*, a spreadsheet, a diary, clock, BBC Basic interpreter, printer interface, and a program to import and export files to and from other computers. There are no disk drives on the Z88. Files do not have to be saved,

but are stored automatically on small match-box sized units that slot into the front of the machine.

3.   A caveat might be expressed that, because the word-processing class had one teacher for five of the seven relevant school terms, the attitudes displayed might owe more to his influence than to use of the technology. This possibility is unlikely, given the very similar attitudes displayed by all the handwriting classes, despite having teachers with teaching styles ranging from the very informal to the relatively authoritarian.

Still, there must be a question mark about the extent of teacher influence here. This will only be clarified in the light of additional studies by others.

4.   The questions about the relative importance of surface revisions concerned: spelling, correct use of capital letters, punctuation, paragraphing, and neatness. The questions about 'meaning' revisions concerned: keeping the reader interested, trying the story out on others, frequent revision, finding exactly the right words, and working out a story-line. The questions concerning the constraints under which they were composing related to: the time allowed, the required length of the story, the subject, the audience, and 'how much you know about the topic?' The three 'test' questions - put in as peripheral to matters of quality - concerned the importance attached to: the cost of the writing paper, the colour of ink used, and the width of the margins. Pupils who did not place at least two of these three questions in the lowest two categories were excluded.

5.   Although the word processor users are the same group - give-or-take a couple of absentees - for this calculation they are treated as two independent groups. A formal statistical objection might be that the second application of the questionnaire could be materially influenced by their memories of the first application.

There are two reasons why this danger has been skirted; one practical and one methodological: (i) relatively long-term use of individual and easily portable laptop computers by whole classes of secondary pupils has only recently become possible, is still extremely rare, and the pupils were, we think, the only class of experienced users in the country at the time, and (ii) it was considered a pretty safe assumption that a 15-minute session during an English lesson a year previously would not materially influence the answers given to the questionnaire second time around.

References

DES. (1989) *English for ages 5 to 16*, Proposals of the Secretary of State for Education and Science and the Secretary of State for Wales. Obtainable from the National Curriculum Council, Information Section, 15-17 New Street, York YO1 2RA.

Duling, R.A. (1985) Word processors and student writing: a study of their impact on revision, fluency, and quality of writing, *Dissertation Abstracts International, 46,* 1823A.

Faigley, Lester & Witte, S. (1981) Analysing Revision, *College Communication and Composition, 32,* pp. 400-414.

Finnegan, R. (1988) *Literacy and Orality,* Oxford: Blackwell.

Fulton G.G. (1988) The effects of word processing and revision patterns on the writing quality of sixth-grade students, *Dissertation Abstracts International,* 50(2).

Haas, C. (1987) How the writing medium shapes the writing process: studies of writers composing with pen and paper and with word processing, *Dissertation Abstracts International,* 49(5), 1081A.

Hawisher, G.E. (1986) The effects of word processing on the revision strategies of college freshmen, *Research in the Teaching of English, 21,* pp. 145-159.

Morrow, J. A. (1989) The effect of keyboarding instruction on middle school students' composition using word processing, *Dissertation Abstracts International,* 50(5), 1203A.

Peacock, M. J. (1988) Hand-writing versus word processed print: an investigation into teachers' grading of English Language and Literature essay work at 16+, *Journal of computer-assisted learning, 4,* pp. 162-172.

Peacock, M. J. & Breese, C. (1990) Pupils with portable writing machines, *Educational Review,* 42(1), pp. 41-56.

Peacock, M.J. (1990) Evaluating the evidence: pupil writers and word processors, *Interchange,* University of Leeds.

Sawford, J. (ed.) (1989) *Promoting Language Development through IT*, National Council for Educational Technology (NCET)

Stein, N.L. (1986) Knowledge and Process in the Acquisition of Writing Skills, in Rothkopf, E.Z.(ed.), *Review of Research in Education,* Washington, DC: American Educational Research Association.

Additional resources

Drage, C. (1988) *On the move,* T. E.S., (28-10-88). p 31.

Dreyfus, H.L, & Dreyfus, S.E. (1984) Putting computers in their proper place: analysis versus intuition in the classroom, *Teachers' College Record,* 85(4), pp. 580-601.

Driver, R. (1987) Changing Conceptions, *Adolescent Development and School Science,* International Seminar at King's College London.

Dudley-Marling, C. & Searle, D. (1989) Computers and language learning: misguided assumptions, *British Journal of Educational Technology*, **20**(1), pp. 41-46.

Appendix: Section B of the questionnaire

Please look through the following list of items. Decide for yourself how important you think each one is in the production of a good story. Put a cross in the column you think best represents how important that item is.

The scale runs from Column One, which means 'Well below average importance', up to Column Five, which means 'Well above average importance'. Column Three is 'Average'.

NO.	ITEMS	1	2	3	4	5
1	Punctuation					
2	Frequently revising					
3	The audience you are writing for					
4	Colour of ink used					
5	How good your spelling is					
6	Finding exactly the right words					
7	How much you know about the topic					
8	Working out the story-line					
9	The cost of the writing paper					
10	Trying the story out on other people					
11	Paragraphing					
12	How long your story has to be					
13	Keeping the reader interested					
14	How much time you have					
15	Correct use of capital letters					
16	The subject you are writing about					
17	How neat your work is					
18	Width of the margins					

7
Collaborative writing using distanced electronic communications

Brent Robinson

The 1980s saw the awakening of interest in electronic communications within the British education system. It was during that decade that developments in the use of electronic communications within commerce and industry were first made available to schools. In one of several Information Technology related initiatives, the Department of Trade and Industry offered each secondary school a free piece of electronic hardware - a 'modem' enabling the school to attach a computer direct to the telephone system for the purpose of sending and receiving electronic data, which in those days was exclusively in the form of typed messages. This allowed schools to access a newly created computer network system - *The Times Network for Schools*, later to become *Campus 2000*. Schools paid a subscription for the use of this service and were allocated an electronic mailbox - their own individual storage area on a large mainframe computer. Here messages could be sent from other school computers and left until the receiving school dialled up the mainframe computer and requested the messages stored in its mailbox to be sent down the line to its own computer screen (and thence to a printer or disk for storage if so required).

Some teachers were very quick to see the potential. There were early experiments with electronic communications involving pen-pal writing (Somekh, 1988). Electronic communication allowed almost immediate transmission of messages and thus overcame the frequently experienced delays of the postal system which had often resulted in crossed letters and/or protracted correspondences which dwindled to nothing as children's enthusiasm evaporated. But unfortunately, these electronic mail exchanges have not necessarily been successful. While communication with distant and culturally remote partners can often excite pupils and provide enriching learning experiences, once the novelty wears off the very speed of information exchange might only hasten the end of a correspondence as children more quickly exhaust their topics of interest.

There were also some experiments with chain story writing. In this, one individual or group starts off a story which is sent to another who writes the following section of narrative. It is then passed back to the original or on to a third party who writes the next part of the story and so on. The model provides children with a new audience and function for creative writing. It can also be accompanied by more transactional writing if pupils are encouraged to communicate with each other to provide responses to what they read or in order to sort out procedural matters. But the format can easily be very open-ended and, like letter-writing, it can easily lose its momentum unless there is a very clear sense of narrative direction and a time-scale for the activity.

At Cambridge University, we established a project funded by the Eastern Arts Association and the National Council for Educational Technology to build upon these early experiences and extend our understanding of what was possible and beneficial with electronic communication in the English classroom. Bearing in mind the need for a strong sense of structure we looked for an appropriate model. In the 18th century the rise of a previous communications network in England, the Post Office, gave impetus to a particular style of narrative writing, the epistolary novel, consisting of an exchange of letters sometimes, but not always, with linking text. The correspondence taken as a whole builds up a story, a story in which the letter-writers are themselves often the leading characters. The form lends itself well to this new electronic communications network too. We created a scenario in which groups of children from six different schools imagined themselves to be teams of explorers sent off on expeditions around the world communicating back home with a retired bed-ridden archaeologist who was funding their travels. Through an exchange of electronic mail between these personae they were to reveal their characters and develop a storyline. The epistolary form was to be used here to enable and regulate the exchange of correspondence and thus to give an overall structure to the compositional phase of the project. But while the epistolary form gave coherence to the whole exchange of fictional correspondence, it was also to facilitate the editing process when pupils would step out of role to consider what they had created and to engage in a redrafting and editorial exercise. Because the narrative text consisted of discrete electronically mailed letters it provided manageable units of text which were short enough to send electronically back and forth for revision and comment.

By including a role play element, we hoped also to build upon the experiences of other pioneers in the field. Chris Warren (1988), who also writes elsewhere in this book, was one of the first in the country to use electronic communications for role play. Electronic mail severely curtails the possible ways in which its users may communicate. Relying heavily on text always delivered in the same format, it gives away little about its senders and their situations. It can thus become a powerful context for imaginative self-projection and role play. By placing the pupils in role in our novel-writing project, we hoped to stimulate their imagination and increase their involvement in the letters they would write. In order not to break the spell, we decided that in the early part of the project the pupils would never communicate out of role. All correspondence would be in character and everything that was transmitted would be considered to be part of the plot.

One of the major attractions of electronic communications is that they can involve pupils in a variety of different communicative roles with a range of new audiences. It is not just other pupils who can be contacted via electronic communications. We were setting up a writing project so why not involve a professional writer? The Arts Council of Great Britain funds a well established subsidy scheme to pay for professional writers to visit schools for literary readings or to run writing workshops. Electronic communications offer the possibility of greater flexibility in arrangements. Schools are no longer confined only to those writers within easy distance from the school. Nor are they constrained by the often very full work schedules of such writers. By giving a writer electronic communication with a school, the writer can communicate with children at a time which is convenient to him or her and even from wherever other work happens to take the writer. Rather than spending a whole day visiting a school, writers can now spend the same amount of time and effort spread over a whole term communicating a little and often with the children, constantly sustaining the work. In our first project, it was the writer himself who determined the precise scenario to fit within the epistolary framework - the bed-ridden archaeologist sending off teams of young explorers through whose correspondence with him he could live vicariously.

In our second project we looked again at the forms of literary collaboration which were possible using electronic communication. The composition of poetry or perhaps short stories can be attractive. Both of these forms again result in manageable short texts which can be easily transmitted electronically to and fro for pupils to comment upon and redraft. At any one time there can be a sufficient number of different poems or stories in the stage of composition, so that several paired groups can be exchanging their text and working on it simultaneously. We decided upon short stories but were again concerned that the activity should have an overall structure to pull together all the different texts being worked on and also to give a sense of development, time scale and a goal to the activity. Again, an existing literary form presented itself to us. Rather than simply producing an anthology of stories we looked to *The Decameron, The Canterbury Tales* and *The Arabian Nights*. Here were stories welded together within some form of fictional context.

We invented a modern version of *The Arabian Nights* in which the children would be more than narrators; they would be protagonists in role. Each group of children from each of the five schools involved became a persona they invented who was now locked in a prison for a deed which the children would have to determine. Although all the prisoners were incarcerated in the same prison they were all in solitary confinement, unable to see each other but able to whisper along the corridor at night when the guards were not listening. This was where electronic communication came in. Electronic mail was to be used to represent the whispered exchanges which took place. One of the prisoners was to be an author whose only crime was that he 'wrote the truth' and so was imprisoned for crimes against the state. Unknown to the pupils, this author was in reality the professional writer we had determined to include in this second project. During the weeks of correspondence, the author encouraged the other prisoners to tell each other stories to pass away the lonely time in their cells. At a predetermined point in the scenario, the author was released from prison but through continued correspondence with the remaining prisoners, he (in reality a female author acting the part of a male writer) persuaded them to discuss with each other the stories they had told and write them up for consideration by the writer's fictional publisher. Once this was done, all the characters stepped out of role and looked at what they had written. Then emulating the narrative model of *The Arabian Nights*, they collaborated to put the stories together and to write an interweaving narrative based on the fictional prison setting they had experienced through role play.

As a result of these two first projects, a number of points arose. It was certainly felt that the particular forms adapted from literary genres proved very useful. They gave a structure to each project providing a framework for the exchange of correspondence and a definite goal to work towards. They also, of course, provided the pupils with an insight into the particular literary genre within which they were working. It would be interesting to explore how well other literary forms lend themselves to the structuring of electronic communication exchanges and in particular what they may contribute to the establishment of appropriate procedures necessary for distanced collaboration, whether or not it involves children in authorship or response, in role or out of it, or their engagement in editorial processes.

The involvement of the writer was another feature which added value to the projects. Both children and teachers valued this source of literary expertise. When the writer was in role, the quality of the imaginative stimulus and feedback to the children provided a great source of motivation. When out of role, the children valued the fact that they were writing for this novel audience or collaborating with such a public expert. But the involvement of writers in such projects is not without its complications. Our first writer felt distinctly uncomfortable with his function. Even though he had once been a language teacher himself, he did not wish to assume this responsibility now. He did not want to be seen to threaten the established position of the teacher with the class. Nor did he feel he should do so given the very different nature of distanced tuition. The writer did not have first-hand experience of the children. He did not know their linguistic strengths and weaknesses. He had no personal knowledge of the children nor (he felt) any way of establishing that personal relationship with each child which every teacher has and upon which the teacher builds.

A face-to-face meeting was arranged for all the teachers and the writer in the project as one means of overcoming potential problems. The aim was to establish working relationships which could then be maintained through electronic communication. (In setting up the project we were mindful of the frequent claim that distanced collaborative relationships cannot be initiated or developed solely through electronic communication. Electronic communications work best, it is argued, when they are predicated upon existing communication networks or when they meet an existing need for communication among an identifiable group of individuals.) Secondly, it was decided that much of the explicit guidance and advice should be channelled through the teachers with private electronic mail to them about the children's writing. Thirdly, when the writer did communicate with the children he would communicate solely in his character role attempting to stimulate their imaginations and assist their writing style through covert means. As the bed-ridden archaeologist of our first project, he received the children's writing as imagined reports from teams of explorers around the world. Thus when, for example, he felt that the descriptive power of writing was wanting, he would write to them in role as the archaeologist reminding them that he was paying for their efforts and living vicariously through them: 'I want to live your expedition through you. That's why you've got to write in detail. IN GREAT DETAIL.'

Our second project resembled the first in its use of a fictional role for the remote expert. Within its prison setting mentioned earlier, the author hid behind the imprisoned male author figure she had created for herself. This enabled her to encourage the pupils as fellow inmates to share information about themselves. Then she began to tell stories and encouraged them to do so. Finally, once she was released from prison, she wrote to them (still in role), persuading them to write up their stories for consideration by her fictional publisher and guiding them in the process.

The same uncertainties shown by our first writer about status, function and relationship when using distanced communication for teaching purposes are not uncommon. As part of our initial teacher training programme at Cambridge University, we wanted to use electronic communication to enable school children to send in their work to our student teachers so the latter could learn at first hand how to respond to children's writing. The student teachers felt uneasy at the idea and so, having learnt from our first project, we decided that a fictional context would be more appropriate for both pupils and student teachers to handle. The student teachers thought up a scenario where they were to be aliens from another planet who had managed to hack into our electronic mail network. They wrote to the pupils asking who they were and what life was like on earth. Then as they received the replies, the student teachers wrote back eliciting more information but all the time setting writing tasks for the children which built upon and developed their previous writing accomplishments.

One of the most exciting realisations arising from our first projects was the power of electronic communications for dramatic involvement. Electronic mail is an opaque medium. It gives very little away about its users. Unlike other forms of communication both face-to-face and distanced (including some of the newer technological media) there are few signifiers available for communication. Everything is communicated solely through text. This text, from whatever source, is received in virtually identical textual font and format on the same computer screen or as hard copy from the same printer. This dependence upon written language can stretch or even tax the linguistic abilities of users of electronic communications, but the same characteristic of the medium also means that nothing is given away about the true nature of the users and this can be employed to advantage. Obvious physical attributes like age, sex, colour or disability are invisible so it becomes much easier to assume a new persona. At the same time, despite the fact that a dialogue may be entered into, there is the opportunity for reflection between utterances. Having received a comment, the recipient can go off line and carefully consider a response before sending it. This allows users to think carefully about how to project themselves with credibility - perhaps using with what appears a natural ease the unfamiliar language and ideas of an assumed persona. The audience for such imaginative self-projection may itself be acting in disguise. But it is also quite possible for those in role to be communicating quite credibly with truly authentic audiences who are not in role but who accept the actors for what they appear to be. This allows the opportunity for pupils to try out with others 'for real' new thoughts and new identities in the knowledge that real responses will be offered.

It is perhaps worth presenting here a note of caution. What messages children send through electronic communications, what messages they are exposed to and how they respond to such messages seem to be important issues for teachers to consider. It can be a surprise to see the extent to which children are willing to suspend their disbelief in imaginary situations in electronic communication contexts. To what extent should they be encouraged to do so, either as transmitters or receivers of messages? Even if no deliberate fictional representation is intended, informal and sometimes uninhibited expression is a feature of the medium. To what extent have teachers a responsibility for the messages their pupils transmit to the very real audience which exists? It is an audience which is capable of sending its own messages sometimes expressing sentiments which teachers may not wish to have articulated in their classrooms. The situation can become confused with a blurring of reality and fiction through the coexistence of authentic and inauthentic statements, characters and situations which sometimes happens.

In our first project, some children were offended by what they detected as a gender bias in comments received from the author. Of course, these comments were expressed in letters received from the author playing the archaeologist - but were the comments those of the author or of his persona, or both? Should this make any difference to the way the children react?

Far more problematic was the very real response one school got from the author when the whole of its written output was rejected. Despite continued attempts at improving the quality of what was being written, the professional writer eventually felt that the standard achieved by one class of pupils was far inferior to that of all the others. They had all been working towards the completion of a book which was to be presented to professional publishing houses for their consideration. Throughout the project, this had been an important motivating force commented upon by both teachers and pupils alike. But towards the end of the redrafting and editing stage, the author still considered the work of one class of pupils detrimental to the quality of the final book they had all produced. He pressed for the removal of all the offending sequences. This eventuality had not been considered by anyone in the project and yet we had been striving for an authentic writing function. Now here was a very real response all too often encountered by writers. If teachers are to allow the real world into the classroom then they must also prepare for its consequences. It will be important to be aware that we may have to teach children how to cope with and respond to a whole set of experiences which until now they have been protected from in school.

Within our projects, some teachers were extremely conscious of the audience with which their children were communicating, and the fact that their children's work was being seen beyond the classroom. Despite the fact that these were collaborative projects, the teachers felt that this was a public medium and that anything communicated electronically was being published. They were thus always concerned about the quality of what was transmitted, no matter what stage of drafting it was at. Of course, we had set up projects in which the correspondence transmitted was to be recorded and used as the basis for a novel. There was thus a perfectly valid reason for careful attention to the formal qualities and the content of anything the pupils transmitted. But while the teachers' own communications often exhibited a considerable degree of informality, they felt that the pupils' work should always display more formally accurate qualities. Working off line, this was easy to effect. The pupils, too, probably felt prompted to write accurately and formally. It remains unclear whether or not greater on-line communication by the pupils would have made them more aware of the informality prevalent among users of the medium, and thus encouraged greater informality from them and a tolerance of inaccuracy. Direct on-line working would be likely to reduce the possibility of intervention by the teacher and hence attempts to satisfy this particular audience as well as the distant audience.

There is a potential tension here between the expectations of teachers about good language use and that language use which the medium encourages. Electronic communications certainly seem to employ different standards of what is acceptable written language use. The style of much electronic linguistic exchange is informal, lying somewhere between the very different stylistic conventions and structure of speech and of writing. This is likely to have implications wherever electronic communications are used in the curriculum. In time, as electronic communications become more widely used, there may need to be a revision of accepted norms of what constitutes good style in relation to expression in this medium or even in relation to writing generally. In the meantime, there could be a positive spin-off if attention to the idiosyncratic style of electronic communication encourages greater language awareness.

It is important to bear in mind that most of what has been discussed here has been in the context of electronic mail upon which most early electronic communications projects were based. What has become evident in the last two years has been a growing interest in and use of other electronic communications media. To some teachers, fax in particular seems attractive. It appears more closely related to familiar print media, being only one step removed from the photocopying of conventional hand-written and printed textual sources. It offers many of the advantages of distanced communication without the disruption to classroom practice. With fax, many conventional writing activities in the classroom can be simply extended to take account of new distant audiences. Hand-written work can be transmitted without the problems of channelling everything through often scarce word-processing facilities. Imaginative textual layouts (including desk-top publishing) and other graphic artwork and images can be transmitted. Copy received by one pupil can be annotated easily by hand and sent back to its author. But there also appear to be disadvantages. Hand-written text and drawing reveal more about the originator than does the uniform printout from other electronic communication. With its graphic ability, children can request photographs and other visual material reducing the uncertainty and lack of concrete realisation which give room for role play and imaginary representation. Children can still be asked to word-process or desk-top publish but the problems of gaining access to computer resources - a necessity with electronic mail - might be so great that little faxed copy is ever computer produced. If this becomes the case, then the motivation we saw in our projects provided by computer use or the sight of computer printout will be lost. So too will the advantages of word-processing for collaborative group writing within the classroom. Distanced collaborative writing may also be confined to the exchange of comment rather than redrafting. With electronic mail, text is received in an electronic form which can be immediately loaded into a word-processor and redrafted before sending back to its originator. Indeed, direct response to children's writing must be in this form or as comments mailed back - it is impossible to annotate a script in the way that teachers conventionally mark and pupils often emulate when asked to respond to each other's work. It would be too laborious to type in a faxed printout to work on or to rewrite by hand a redraft of someone else's work. Instead with fax, collaborators may be induced to confine their activities to editorial comment and annotation of the sender's text.

Of course, such considerations may prove in time to be immaterial. It is still too early to tell. In any case, every medium has its appropriate uses. At Cambridge we have now set up *The Distant Muse Project* in which seven groups of schools are exploring further some of the issues raised in this chapter via a mixture of media - electronic mail, conferencing, fax and even telephone and post! Satellite transmission is also beginning to feature in distanced communication. Hopefully in due time we will be in a clearer position to assess the relative benefits of each technology in relation to the value of distanced communication in the curriculum.

References

Somekh, B. & Groundwater-Smith, S. (1988), Take a Balloon and a Piece of String, in D. Smith (ed.), *New Technologies and Professional Communications in Education*. National Council for Educational Technology, London.

Warren C. (1988), *Live Adventuring*. Derbyshire Educational Support Centre for IT.

8
Computer-based information-stream simulations: their impact on language and thinking

Chris Warren

Computer-based information-flow simulations are nothing new. Eight years ago when I first encountered computers in an educational context, on a training event, I experienced the newsroom simulation *Bomb*, published by Shropshire Local Education Authority. I remember how gripped I became. Every minute or so the story was updated - the tragedy of the Hyde Park terrorist bombing - and we were all caught up in the dynamism of news-on-the-move. It was fundamentally exciting; it felt as if the bulletins coming off the printer were real, as if the bombing had actually taken place that morning. We worked through the coffee break and into the lunch hour, not wanting to stop.

However, the general concept of a computer delivering measured quantities of information to a group prepared to process it seemed largely unexploited, apart from the now ubiquitous 'newsroom' events. I do not consider newsroom simulations passé - they will always be useful in the classroom - yet the potential power of the computer as a kind of tap, dripping information into the stream of human thought and action was not much developed.

I became fascinated by this field, was sure the computer offered something special - I had felt it myself doing *Bomb*. You might ask, 'Why use a computer?' It is true that information sequencing and control can be achieved without the use of a machine - one can read a book, or watch a film or play, following the author's or producer's thoughts in the process. However, computers offer some unique possibilities that go far beyond the simple linear sequence embodied in most books, films and paper-based newsroom simulations:

- the rate of flow can be exactly controlled;
- the sequence of information can be controlled;
- branching in the script can be achieved, establishing unique routes through the information, determined by the group using the computer, by random functions, or by some mathematical rule;
- interaction with the computer can be incorporated in the script so that users alter the nature of the information in some way.

The chief advantage, however, is that all the above is controlled and managed by a machine - no poor teacher is caught up in the process, and because there is no overt human agency involved (the printer suddenly begins to work as if prompted by a remote telex operator) it is easy to suspend disbelief, to become seduced by the realism of the messages.

Other factors contribute to the sense of realism: society tends to make little gods out of computers, the new miracle workers, and therefore the information they disgorge has an exaggerated, unwarranted authority. This fact can be exploited in education and training to enhance the realism of an information-flow simulation. After the event, issues related to the sometimes spurious authority of computer information can be raised.

In many contexts in the real world information **would** come through a computer, so to use a computer for that function is to give it a completely natural and credible role in the drama of a classroom simulation. In this way the computer not only handles fractured information efficiently, it also, as a spin-off, invests it with power.

This paper sets out to consider the impact on language, and the thought-processes represented by language, of computer-based information-flow. I want to explore and illustrate some alternatives to the familiar newsroom simulation, and look at the effect of these on individuals. I will begin by describing two simulations I have written.

Hijack was written in 1986. It consists of two scripts. The first, a newsroom simulation containing a series of news bulletins, is used by a class to create the front page of a newspaper. The second, a special script from an imagined Crisis Control Centre, delivers top secret information to a group of students adopting the roles of the Cabinet. Their script is very different from the one in the newsroom: it will branch according to decisions made by the Cabinet at crucial junctions in the crisis - they are handling a serious *Hijack* incident. The two groups, the Newsroom(s) and the Cabinet, work independently, have totally different information at their disposal. They are forced to interact, however, through Press Conferences, held every quarter of an hour, where one member of the Cabinet, the Press Secretary, has to face the Press.

The effect of this combination of news that is received passively by reporters from the computer, and the 'real' news delivered by the Press Secretary (the Cabinet make decisions that directly alter the news!) is explosive in its power. Anyone witnessing the white-knuckled excitement and tension of a typical Cabinet is immediately impressed by the 'grip' of the event and the almost unbearable pressure experienced by the group making decisions.

The reporters find the event equally stimulating as making the Press Secretary divulge any significant news at all, takes aggressive and clever questioning. They are caught up in stormy Press Conferences that are part performance and part vigorous contest.

Students emerge tired but exhilarated, saying the occasion was, 'The best thing I ever did in school'.

Why? What makes this technique so compelling? The answer lies, I think, in language: the way communication is put under a press and the power of the verbal contests that go on, both in the Cabinet, around the editors' tables and between the Press Secretary and reporters at Press Conferences.

In the language activities of *Hijack*, the energy level is high because the computer is used tangentially, as an information **source,** not as a primary focus of attention. Participants do not do the social equivalent of watching television (typical of so much computer use); they talk to each other, make eye contact, argue, laugh, scream, agree - all away from the computer. This is a crucial point - just because the technology seems to **demand** attention it does not necessarily follow that we should sit in front of the screen gawping, or that this is the best way to use computers in the classroom, despite the siren calls of beautiful graphics and other sophistications.

Hijack acts as a powerful stimulus to language, but that language goes through several transformations in the course of reaching a final form as a newspaper article.

For the Cabinet the information input starts as a print-out from the computer; this is carried away from the machine to be read and discussed. Here the rule is that each new bulletin is **read aloud.** This changes the essential nature of the language, from potentially static, lifeless, impersonal and solitary (the print-out) to dynamic, human, personal and public. The language picks up aspects of the reader's personality in the act of being read aloud and, in effect, becomes full communication, a dramatic utterance like a line from a play.

At one of the early trials this process was beautifully illustrated, and the experience at most *Hijack* events is similar. On this occasion, the member of the Cabinet detailed to read the bulletins became increasingly tense and excited as the simulation progressed, and his sense of urgency communicated itself infectiously to the rest of the group. The event **was** exciting to watch. Had the first information been read silently on screen, had the print-out been passed around to be read silently, or even had the bulletins been read in a bored tone of voice, the collective sense of urgency would not have found expression.

In the process of being read aloud not only is the information given life and colour, it is also **broadcast.** All the members of the Cabinet receive the information simultaneously, they all participate in the same act of assimilation.

In *Hijack* the information is easy to absorb; it is narrative and sequential, not cryptic in nature and does not need to be theorised over unduly. After the reading there is a reaction from the Cabinet and a transformation ensues. All new information requires processing because of the regular Press Conferences. These dictate the nature of the transformation: the rules of secrecy imply levels of distortion and concealment that force participants to formulate and reformulate their statements. This powerful oral editing process is aimed at achieving some collectively acceptable version, sensitive to moral considerations (do the Cabinet want to lie?) and the two conflicting pressures: to keep information back and to publish it. Eventually the Press Secretary writes down or notes what the consensus is. Meanwhile the information continues to flood in, so these processes actually happen in parallel, overlapping and interweaving.

After about ten minutes there is an alarm signal and the Cabinet are faced with a decision. At the base of the screen a clock begins to count down the number of seconds left to decide. Some decisions are given three minutes, some eight. When it happens for the first time there is general panic. Voices struggle to assert themselves. Everyone seems to want to speak at the same time.

When urgent decisions are required in a specified time there may be one of two reactions. The first is to opt out of the discussion phase altogether, perhaps steered by one dominant voice, and plump for one choice straight away. 'Let's push 2!' says the voice and the group assent, only vaguely assimilating the arguments. The second reaction is to become so bogged down in dispute that no decision is possible, the time expires, and the situation passes beyond the control of the Cabinet.

To prevent both problems a rule was instituted that a vote must be taken and a decision entered only when 30 seconds remain on the screen clock. Before that time the issues must be fully considered, both the options that are to be rejected and the one chosen course of action. That way the instant button-push impulse is deferred and real debate has a chance to emerge. Voting effectively ends the debate.

The constraints detailed above - and remember that participants are working under extreme pressure - produce some quite startling exchanges. Language becomes excited, forceful and efficient and lengthy expansion of opinion disappears.

Discursive thought is a very difficult mode - a certain maturity is needed, especially where participants are required to consider arguments that directly oppose their own. Yet Cabinets involved in *Hijack* regularly display an astonishing ability to explore arguments against their own chosen course of action. This might be prompted by the screen displays, which give a summary of 'points for' and 'points against' and thus encourage students to weigh up the odds.

It may also be stimulated by the genuinely counterbalanced nature of the decisions in *Hijack* which are written so that there are no easy solutions: every option has its pros and cons.

Whatever the reason, I have observed discussion during these Cabinet sessions of a quality that I had been quite unable to create in the ordinary classroom: the combination of deadline pressure, excitement and a fairly formal set of rules leads to the production of language and thought that goes far beyond the level achieved by the students in their normal setting.

Profound personal discoveries are made during this process, as evidenced in many, many pieces of writing after the event. Sometimes the exact moment where a student becomes personally aware can be observed: at one event at a school near Chesterfield, Derbyshire, a member of the Royal Family had just been discovered to be on the flight. The plane was grounded at Birmingham Airport and believed to be on fire. The terrorists had escaped with two hostages, commandeering a helicopter in the process: they were finally cornered when the helicopter developed engine trouble and landed near the M6.

The Cabinet were then faced with the following decision:

DO YOU RECOMMEND THAT WE

(1) SEND IN THE ARMY

POINTS FOR: Quick solution to what may be a long-drawn-out affair

POINTS AGAINST: Likely to cause the deaths of the hostages

(2) NEGOTIATE

POINTS FOR: Best way to achieve a non-violent solution

POINTS AGAINST: Unlikely to persuade these desperate people

(3) CONCEDE TERRORIST DEMANDS

POINTS FOR: May lead to release of hostages

POINTS AGAINST: Encourages terrorism

A girl on the Cabinet suddenly became outraged that a number of the hawkish boys opposite were recommending a military solution to the *Hijack*, despite the warning that it might cause a bloodbath. With considerable passion she argued for the right of all people to live, that the number was not a relevant factor, that all people are precious irrespective of their rank in society.

It was an astonishing and moving performance, largely because it was so unexpected, and the person most taken aback was the girl herself! The simulated crisis had precipitated her into discovery of her own morality and at the same time shown up the bankrupt state of the boys' morals: they had no reply to her most persuasive line, 'What if it was your brother or your mother on that plane? Just because there are only two of them doesn't mean we can risk killing them.'

That particular moment of crisis regularly leads to egalitarian debate - why should the decisions be altered just because Prince Edward is on the plane? Sometimes the voice of political expediency is heard when students realise the career-suicide of being involved with a Cabinet which made decisions that led to the death of a member of the Royal Family!

All the time, the computer sits in the corner pushing out more and more information, never allowing the pace to flag, keeping the pressure and the sense of realism high. A measure of the degree to which Cabinets are seduced by the realism can be drawn from the following anecdote.

Highfields School in Matlock, Derbyshire had organised a very ambitious event involving the entire Year 10. All twelve of the Cabinet were gathered in a Deputy's office: outside, 200 students busily compiled the front pages of newspapers, and recorded radio and TV news, prompted by a continuous stream of information from twelve separate computers, set up in each of the classrooms in use. The Press conferences on this occasion were frightening, attended by 40 reporters: dauntingly intimidating for the poor Press Secretary. The atmosphere was generally highly charged.

It is often possible to improvise around the script: I noticed that the office the Cabinet were using had a phone. At the appropriate moment in the script, I set up a stooge in the staffroom, told him to use a heavy accent, and to repeat a set phrase whatever was said. Then in my role as Civil Servant I came in with the news that direct negotiation with the terrorists was possible. The Home Secretary took the call but returned to the table convinced that she had been attached to a tape-recorder because of the repetition. I suggested politely that the difficulty might have arisen because the terrorists did not speak English; they were reading a set phrase off a piece of paper.

At this point a girl in the Cabinet spoke up: 'I speak German, let me take the phone.' (We had discovered that a German woman was on the plane earlier.)

Somewhat flummoxed I said that I would see what I could do and rushed out. As luck would have it, believe it or not, a German teacher was on a free period at that very moment and she immediately agreed to help. A minute or so later I returned announcing that the German terrorist was willing to talk. The girl, who had spent a year in Vienna, bravely took the phone before a hushed and incredulous Cabinet. Not one person in the room doubted at that second that the simulation was real, not one person even wondered how on earth I had done it! They listened to their colleague in awed and uncomprehending silence, then continued with Cabinet business with renewed vigour when she returned to translate the conversation!

Away from the Cabinet, the pressure of producing a newspaper to a set deadline can prove equally gripping, and many students report an increased awareness of the whole process: they have enjoyed the team work and the occasional opportunities to exercise leadership.

The second simulation I want to discuss, *Murder*, was also written in 1986, and refined over the succeeding months. Derived from a simple card clue game, the computer delivers bulletins every minute or so purporting to come from detectives on the scene. These include statements from witnesses, examination of the scene of the crime, reports from Forensic Scientists on the state of the body, reports from detectives searching the flat of the deceased, and a mass of other evidence, not all of it relevant.

The narrative sequence is completely disrupted and the 'clues' are quite often cryptic. Pupils work in squads of five. Each squad has a runner whose job it is to fetch the latest bulletin. Bulletins must be read out before being filed, or passed around, or displayed (squads are given complete freedom as to how they process the information once it has been printed).

The task, reconstruct the narrative order and rebuild the story from sometimes fragmentary evidence, is a daunting undertaking: the computer never lets up - information **pours** in, threatening to overwhelm the group. There is pressure on everyone to find some form of organisation, if only to survive the information overload.

Usually there is a period of about 20 minutes when the dominant feeling is one of bewilderment, and then something begins to happen - a certain intellectual excitement creeps into the language exchanges: hypotheses begin to form, group members become increasingly animated.

The process lasts about 90 minutes. Each squad will by then have already been asked to give a verbal report to a senior officer (usually the local community policeman, commandeered for the occasion). Finally each group must give an account of the last hours of the murder victim, and say who the chief suspect is, and why.

I was always delighted by the way this particular simulation went - it has been used countless times with adults on in-service training courses and seems to be as successful with them as with any pupils. I could not quite define why the computer's role was so effective. What is it doing that makes the event suddenly *take* with participants in that way? What are the language processes involved? Why do participants become so animated?

I have had the chance to watch *Murder* many times and I believe something very significant is taking place. What I have been observing is not collaborative talk, but collaborative **thought**.

Questions are often asked about language and the half-hidden processes of power and control that take place through verbal exchanges. I would now like to focus on the processes of thinking in such contexts, how a group faced with a common puzzle find the mental strategies required for its solution. *Murder*, quite fortuitously, stimulates shared thinking. The creation, in that process, of an efficient collective 'mind', causes the mental excitement I mentioned earlier - enough intellectual energy to keep a group of Year 10 pupils working flat out for 90 minutes non-stop. What follows is an exploration of the process.

First we must examine more closely the nature of the material in *Murder* and *Lost* (quite different from *Hijack*). There are **four** elements to the scripts, apart from one or two direct puzzles (a water-logged message needing deciphering, a torn up letter needing re-assembling):

- There is a narrative, a story, embedded in the script, but the sequence has been completely disrupted. Squads have to re-establish the original sequence.
- Parts of the narrative are omitted: they can only be re-created by inference and supposition based on the clues.

- There are frequent examples of fragmentary or incomplete data. Squads have to interpret these hints; expand the 'encoded' data so that the gaps are filled.
- Red herrings are introduced, again with both narrative order disturbed and fragmentary data. Squads not only have to re-construct the rogue story, they also have to evaluate its authenticity or relevance, and find some way of eliminating it so that the true story may emerge.

The information above predicates a whole series of language operations and uses, involves a range of language codes and strategies, but more than anything it demands concentration, deduction and interpretation - in a word, **thought**. It is possible to observe a sequence of processes that goes roughly like this:

1. Transmission
2. Assimilation and exchange
3. Data assembly: compilation: selection: emphasis: organisation
4. Further assimilation
5. Interpretation and theory
6. Selection and emphasis; modification of theory
6. Re-transmission

Expressed diagrammatically the model might look a little like Fig. 1. Here the thinking and language activities are closely tied together - it would be impossible to disentangle them. The first step in the process, Transmission of Data has already been discussed. Before the computer even begins to pour out information each squad has documents, called 'focus documents', to look at. These consist, typically, of a map and some other pieces of diagrammatic data.

Focus documents are aptly labelled: they perform a vital function in promoting communal concentration. Squads cluster round the map; eyes seem to lock onto the diagram; staring at the map goes on for far longer than might be expected; and tactile contact with the map - a finger will trace a road, or someone will simply touch it, - seems to aid rapid mental orientation and co-ordination.

The tactile phenomenon is particularly noticeable with younger children but persists throughout the age range. It seems to be a stage in thinking where body, eye and mind co-ordinate, and is thus a vital component of collaborative thought.

Watching a squad round the map one realises that not only are members locating themselves individually, the group is becoming collectively 'tuned in' (observable in many human contexts, from the mental/spiritual concentration of churchgoers on the cross above the altar, to the tactile sharing of family photographs). It is an excellent preparation for the more sophisticated interactions that occur when data begins to flow in from the computer.

THE THINKING CYCLE

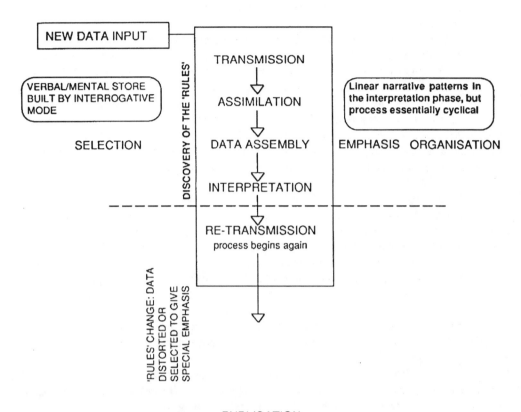

Fig. 1.

Now information starts to come from the machine in printed form and is, as I said before, **broadcast** to the group through being read aloud. This reading needs to be clear and efficient (each squad should have at least one good reader). Thus, all the collected thinkers receive the information simultaneously at least once, irrespective of what they do with the data subsequently.

In the process of transmission the data goes through a change, from printed to oral form, and also becomes invested with human characteristics as a by-product of being read aloud. Receiving information through **listening** stimulates cerebral activities that are different from **reading:** it powerfully reinforces the latter.

So the group has received the data. It now needs to assimilate the new facts. The following assimilation strategies can be observed:

- communication conducted almost exclusively through questions
- selection and emphasis of data
- display of printouts and constant re-reading
- data insertion into the current data-fund
- early sequencing of data
- early interpretations

Almost immediately the next stage begins: **assembly**. This is accompanied by a quite unexpected language phenomenon noted above: almost all the dialogue switches to interrogative form!

Questions are asked **almost every second** and they continue throughout the simulation with the same startling frequency except in the interpretation phase. Why is this? Why does it so often prove the most efficient form of communication in this context? What diverse functions do these questions have?

Interrogative mode perhaps has a strong social appeal because questions suggest ideas, whereas statements dominate, and questions invite participation both by form and by implication. Most questions encourage a sense of equality in a group. However, beyond its social attractiveness, the use of questions has great advantages for the team's problem-solving efficiency and this is what I would like to focus on.

It might be useful to categorise the question forms: they fall roughly into at least five categories.

There are phatic or rhetorical questions, seeking confirmation rather than information, often in the form of statements marked by an interrogative tag: 'Drayton went upstairs, **didn't he?'** As a function of **language** these forms of question maintain the flow of communication, support and bolster talk, fill the spaces where the conversations are in neutral. As a feature of **thought**, however their function is **assembly**: by constant repetition, a group assembles a data-pool. This pool of collectively-held information needs constant refreshment to make it current in the team-mind, so rhetorical questions that do not seek an answer beyond an 'mmm' or 'yes' serve to lift data-items to the surface, or to insert data into the working data-pool.

The form of the rhetorical question or its frequency can also mark out certain data-items as special. The group cannot keep every fact in play at once; it must *select*. Beyond selection there is **emphasis**, where a sub-group of data-items is given particular scrutiny. All these processes can be traced clearly in the pattern of questions asked by the group. They form the necessary intellectual groundwork for the take-off phase of theoretical thinking.

Another category of question is the enquiry that demands a real answer, which cannot be responded to by a 'yes' or 'no'. In this group are the *wh-* forms - 'what', 'why', 'when', 'which' and 'where'. A *wh-* question demands direct cerebral response, it demands that you think!

Even if you do not reply to the question, if you have heard a *wh-* question, you will be obliged to think. It forces exploratory or innovatory thinking on the group as a whole. The iterative rhetorical forms discussed above, which ask more for confirmation than new thinking, stimulate a different mode of mental activity: a monitor mode. In monitor mode the thinker attempts to check another's thinking rather than push out the boundaries of the whole group's mental explorations. When innovatory thinking is taking place the question forms mark out that fact, and this often precedes the formulation of tentative hypotheses. Innovatory thinking represents the real *work* of the group: it is embarked upon by a temporary group leader, a bit like a leading runner or a front-flying Canada goose taking on the lead for a short while. The innovator is watched and monitored by the rest of the team and her/his researches become part of the data-pool.

If the innovator genuinely demands an answer the question will be repeated as in this example:

A: Where's 10 Gladstone Close?... PAUSE

A: Where's 10 Gladstone Close?... LONG PAUSE

A: 10 Gladstone Close?...Where's 10 Gladstone Close? VOICE RISING IN INSISTENCE

B: There's 10 Gladstone Close...

(Quotations from *Murder* running at Long Eaton Community School, 1988)

Here you can see how the iterative process works in the extreme repetition of a key data-item - altogether four repetitions, and the reply couched so that it too is a repetition. The communal mind is thus thoroughly alerted to the fact in question - it is established as having emphasised status. In its selectivity, communal thinking sometimes resembles the individual consciousness: when listening to the radio we can blank out the sound of traffic outside, or other distractions, we can focus our attention. The communal mind seems to do the same - there is no attempt to keep all the data in play.

Some questions set out to **organise** the data-pool, to categorise and connect data-items. This process runs in parallel with selection and emphasis and is a powerful prelude to hypothetical thinking.

Other questions are, in reality, power-moves where a dominant personality takes over the management of the group's thinking through a series of directed rhetorical questions, the answers to which are already known. (This in its overt form is the strategy employed by teachers, of course!) A pattern emerges after three or four such questions and the group may become aware that there is a coup underway, that power is being usurped! Question form is chosen because the power-moves then are half-disguised, appear polite. If the person in question is in fact a powerful thinker the results can sometimes be good; but the thinking rapidly falls away from collaborative thought. The majority of the team are sidelined into monitor mode and cannot participate in innovatory thinking unless they are prepared to follow the powerful lead set by the dominant member. Their scope is restricted, and should the set course be misguided, the group will have difficulty eliminating the mistake. In some contexts, therefore, the emergence of dominant leaders can have a less than positive effect!

Where true team-thinking occurs, monitor mode and innovatory thinking remain in balance and the maximum flexibility is thus maintained.

Having assembled a common data-pool and compiled, selected, organised and emphasised data within it, the group can begin constructing a working hypothesis.

A speaker will command the attention of the others in the group with a statement such as: 'I know what happened...' following it with a reconstruction of the narrative.

While this is taking place the rest of the group go silent. Attention is riveted on the speaker, as by this stage they are more conscious of the group than the individual, and efficient communication acquires a high premium. This feature of the hypothetical stage is quite remarkable - in a group that is working well there does not seem to be the usual jostling for the spotlight or problems with turn-taking, or interruptions. It seems that, as the group thinking develops, so the value of individual contributions goes up. The speaker here is animated by unusual levels of excitement, eyes bright, voice louder than usual, gesture exaggerated. The enunciation of the theory involves rehearsal of parts of the common data-pool - this has the effect of raising the data to the surface again and because the data is held in common, the thinking team has the means to monitor and inspect the theory for flaws. Mental excitement shows on the listeners' faces and when the speaker has finished there is often a chorus of interruptions, a swift struggle to establish who will be the next lead-thinker. Monitors now modify the current theory or take the lead and launch their own version.

If the theoretical stage is attempted prematurely, with an inadequate data-pool sometimes the **joke-hypothesis** emerges. This is constructed out of fabricated data with impossibly far-fetched conclusions. The result is usually an explosion of laughter; tension in the group seems to be reduced; a greater flexibility and adventurousness is introduced into the thinking. The effect is often akin to brain-storming: sometimes the joke-hypothesis sparks off a serious line of thought. It is more common when adults are using the simulation, perhaps because they are more familiar with the genre, the classic explanations of famous detectives, and therefore feel the itch to send-up the whole thing. By and large in my observations, the joke-hypothesis is positive in its effect and serves among other things as a rehearsal for the true enunciations of theory that are to come.

The language used begins to reflect the structures of logic - it would be a good test of Bernstein's 'restricted code' theories! - and forms such as this are common:

FACT STATEMENT ... 'so'... INTERPRETATION

Meanwhile, throughout, information continues to pour out of the computer, indefatigably, so that the processes outlined above fall into a continuous cycle.

The above represents a first attempt to analyse the phenomena associated with information-stream simulations. It is best to try them out; observe first-hand. The use of a computer as an inspiration, as a tool in the classroom, well away from the true focus of the activity, is something that has proved to be unexpectedly powerful. There is so much more to explore with strategies like this, especially at a time when the dazzling potential of the technology continues mesmerically, way beyond sound theoretical and practical applications of its wizardries.

Minds need ways into data; they need to find real reasons for absorbing and manipulating facts; they cannot cope with unlimited quantities or connections that are too tenuous. We should remember those lessons, as the computer woos us towards its brave new world, and set about adapting the sheer power of the machine to meet our own agendas. I have attempted to follow those precepts in *Hijack* and *Murder*, and the information-stream simulations that followed them.

9
Computer discourse: language imprisoned or empowered?

Francis Curtis

'Thirty years ago, Marseilles lay burning in the sun, one day'

This arresting first sentence of Dickens' novel *Little Dorrit* plays with the reader's understanding of the word 'burning'. Is the city literally so hot that people, objects - burn? Or is this some indication of an emotional, spiritual condition? The reader, within a page or so, has both possibilities enlarged as Dickens' cinematic prose moves to 'a villainous prison' in Marseilles. Here, entombed, Monsieur Rigaud exclaims 'To the devil with this Brigand of a Sun that never shines in here!': the title of the chapter, 'Sun and Shadow' ushers in both metaphorical and literal resonances. As I glance to the left of my computer keyboard I take in the cover of a familiar software reference manual with its appetising orange fruit logo and 'APRICOT SOFTWARE GEM DESKTOP' heading. There is a line drawing of a simple desk underneath and the introduction page beguiles me with this paragraph:

> Instead of presenting you with information on your screen in an unhelpful style (as you'll find with most other computers), GEM desktop does it in a much more friendly way. Its whole concept is based on making your computer act in a similar way to a normal office desk. Just like a desk it has a work surface, drawers, files, folders and even desk accessories such as a clock and calculator.

In both the literary (Dickens) and computer (Apricot GEM) discourses I recognise metaphor at work. The purpose of this chapter will be to take a close look at the highly metaphorical language of computer discourse through a consideration of, for example, advertisements, and to link this with education and English teaching: I will present some lessons I taught this year (March 1991) with a Year 10 class to share my experience of trying to explore with them the limitations and liberations of computer discourse. Naturally, CAL and National Curriculum Statements of Attainment are involved! By outlining my experience of exploring some of the characteristics of computer discourse both in theory and in classroom practice I hope to stimulate more discussion and schemes of work on the relationships between language and computers in education. The starting point for this chapter is what I take to be a crucial difference between the use of metaphor in literary discourse and that in computer discourse: in the former, the reader invariably recognises the ambivalence, contingency and familiar provisional nature of the metaphor. If you like, a **critically aware** acknowledgement that the context is fictive and imaginative and that one's commitment to it is aesthetic rather than literal and mimetic. In contrast, the language of everyday life - which takes in the manufacture, deployment, usage and advertising of computers - is also metaphorical, but much more frequently our stance towards it is **uncritical**: we are simply unaware of the *Metaphors We Live By* (Lakoff & Johnson, 1980). This contract is not lost on the computer marketing industry, however: the writers of software manuals and advertising copywriters have developed a fascinating metaphorical landscape for us to explore, strewn with acorns, apples, apricots, mice, garbage, trash cans and viruses. This initial part of the chapter charts some features of the computer in education terrain in order to offer a particular slant on the significance of metaphor.

Close encounters of the computer kind

Teaching staff, students and pupils find themselves, to varying degrees, in a technological environment which is changing at an ever increasing rate. 'There needs no ghosts, my lord, come from the grave/To tell us this': yet Hamlet's 'wild and whirling words', as the drama unfolds, reveal a condition of being in Denmark rather than a trite point about 'human nature'. It is a condition which he interrogates critically and it eventually costs many lives. In somewhat similar but less dramatic vein there is some point in examining the condition of being an English teacher, student or pupil in the computer environment. From a curriculum point of view the advent of computers in schools and colleges has brought three types of innovation: content, organisation and market innovation. National Curriculum requirements, through Statements of Attainment at different levels (to which I will return) have legislated for Information Technology in English classroom 'content' with post-16 developments also subject to reform proposals.

These forms of curriculum innovation have a pervasive impact upon our work with other staff as well as upon those we teach. The impact differs depending upon many factors and is distinctive with respect to our work in English in primary classrooms or secondary English Departments or post-compulsory English. Nevertheless, we are grappling, on a day-to-day basis, with two major professional areas with respect to computer-related learning. The first concerns our decision-making responsibilities in the face of computer technology and the second involves an awareness of what learning English in a computer context demands. The two, clearly, are related because responsible decision-making and taking is informed by knowledge, experience and theory. Whether individually or corporately, in a departmental or curriculum team, questions have to be asked - and answered - about computer usage. These can be pressingly pragmatic 'Have I (and my pupils) the time, space and close support to make use of a computer?' but also puzzling and philosophical, 'What are our relationships with the computer?' The latter question, nagging and often unresolved because we lack the time to discuss it, often acts as a kind of brake on our daily practices. Implicitly, if not often explicitly, answers to it inform our daily decisions in planning lessons to develop learning in English and determine our use of computer equipment.

This fundamental question of our relationships with computers has received, and continues to receive, attention from the dual viewpoints of popular culture and education. We need to consider both. The behavioural envelope of schooling and institutionalised education is obviously permeated by all manner of cultural influences, computer technology included. Acute observers of the media such as Marshall McLuhan (1964) and Neil Postman (1987) have both been consistent for the past 20 to 30 years in arguing that technology is inseparable from the values of the culture which produces and uses it and that electronic-based cultures define modes of perceiving and acting in the world:

> McLuhan has developed a theory that goes like this: The new technologies of the electronic age, notably television, radio, the telephone, and computers make up a new environment. The idea that these things, TV and the rest, are just tools that men can use for better or worse depending on their talents and moral strengths - that idea is idiotic to McLuhan. The new technologies, such as television, have become a new environment. This radically alters the entire way people use their five senses, the way they react to things, and therefore their entire lives and the entire society.
>
> Wolfe, (1968) p.41

Television and computer technologies, so the argument runs, are not added on to the human environment. They are powerfully constitutive of that environment and change its reality in radical ways. The other Michael Jackson (BBC's *Open the Box* producer) says of his experience with the programme, which put a camera on top of the TV set to record audience reaction: 'What I learned was that people **lived** in front of the TV. They walked in and out of the room, ate their dinner, talked. And sometimes they really concentrated, really watched hard. Their response was sophisticated' (*The Independent on Sunday*, 26 May 1991). As with television and video, so with computers in our popular culture as active shapers and moulders of our environments: the moral questions of the Gulf Conflict (one-sided massacre or war?) are inseparable from the computer networks which controlled the hi-tech weaponry of the allied airforces. The contact which pupils and staff have in doctors' surgeries with keyboards, monitors and print-out prescriptions is as familiar as their contact with computerisation in banks, shops, telephones: all are well-honed examples of our citizen involvement with computer technology.

It would be strange indeed if teachers of English did not perceive a line of continuity running through the fourth, 'invisible wall' of the classroom which connects pupils as learners with pupils as young citizens. Of course, we do. The relationships which we have as teachers and pupils of English with computers is massively intriguing. How aware are we of the ideology and language of computer discourse, for instance? Do pupils have a critical and informed view on these issues? Does our curriculum planning include giving our pupils and students opportunities to work with the ideology and language of computer discourse?

Machines and metaphors

The path I am taking over this computer in education terrain has led us towards a consideration of the relationships we have, as staff, pupils and students, with technology and computers in particular. One way of considering these relationships is in terms of role where management theory on human relations can help us. The interactions between a machine - the computer - and a human being entail role relationships of a particular kind. Effective personnel management is often achieved by people who are both aware of and able to put into practice insights offered by role theory. For instance, if I am clear (in my role as English teacher) about who constitutes my immediate role set (e.g. pupils, department colleagues, Head of Department) and also the role boundaries (the limits of authority and accountability) then I am likely to manage my professional relationships more effectively than I would have done otherwise. The particular notion of role boundary is positively transferable to thinking about my role as a teacher or pupil in relation to the role of the machine in my teaching or learning.

The daily experience of our professional teaching lives illustrates quite clearly that role boundaries shift and change, are permeable, can be held firm in one situation but not in another. However, this experience does not detract from the value to be gained from establishing, through analysis, how and why this happens. Ihde (1975) has proposed a useful analysis of the role relations between humans and machines along a continuum of 'transparency' and 'opacity': the more a machine functions in the role of bodily extension (for instance pen, garden fork) the more it is transparent; the more this device functions as separate from us the more opaque it is. The analysis proceeds in degrees along this imaginary continuum. The first stage, as represented for example by driving a car, identifies the human with the machine through bodily sensation: the driver can perceive movement, temperature, visual field and so on in such a way that the machine is 'transparent'. In the second stage (for example watching television or using the telephone) the machine recedes more but is still part of the user's bodily environment. The third, 'opaque' stage is reached when the human is divided off from the machine because the machine is perceived as separate, with its own identity. An example of this is the computer, in Ihde's analysis.

I have now come to a fork in our path: one leg of the fork offers us the computer as separate, with its own identity, the other offers us the computer simply as a machine extension of hands and fingers. Let us follow the first leg of the fork.

Theodore Roszak (1986) writes interestingly about the folklore of the computer, echoing Arthur C. Clarke's dictum 'Any sufficiently advanced piece of technology is indistinguishable from magic'. Like a mythical creature, the computer takes on a cult following and distinctions between what is human and what is machine are lost in the flux of what Roszak calls 'an undergrowth of advertising hype, media fictions and commercial propaganda' (Roszak, (1986), p.ix). Advertising and commercial propaganda form part of a computer discourse which Year 10 students have the motivation to work with, as I show later in this chapter. Here, Roszak insists on the need for teachers and pupils to be aware of boundaries:

> The burden of my argument is to insist that there is a vital distinction between what machines do when they process information and what minds do when they think. At a time when computers are being intruded massively on schools, that distinction needs to be kept plainly in view by teachers and students alike. But thanks to the cult like mystique that has come to surround the computer, the line that divides mind from machine is being blurred. Accordingly, the powers of reason and imagination which the schools exist to celebrate and strengthen are in danger of being diluted with low grade mechanical counterfeits.

The 'cult like mystique' which Roszak mentions is achieved through language drawn from a variety of discourse contexts within the computer culture: advertisements, manuals and operating instructions for instance, in numerous settings - books, magazines, television transmissions and so on. This language is part of a cultural process which enacts social meanings and practices, and which represents computers, falsely, as conscious beings. The computer culture, understood in both intellectual and anthropological senses, influences language usage profoundly but this process is frequently unnoticed, escaping conscious attention; hence the ideas of magic and masquerade, of separate identities and blurred boundaries. The agent is language and an explicit exploration of it a motivating and valuable activity for teachers and learners in English. Daniel Chandler (1990) has recorded his views on the role of language in computer culture in these terms:

> It is important to insist that **there is no information in computers, only data.** Human beings create information by interpreting the evidence of their senses and through negotiating with other human beings. This is no mere semantic quibble: the language of the computer culture threatens to redefine the world in its own terms. Manuals and users talk of 'storing' information on computers and 'retrieving' it from them. Computers, even more than books, masquerade as 'containers' of information and divorce information from human action and a social context, and thus from meaning.
>
> In order to support the needs of the machine we are encouraged to become computers ourselves...this is seductive propaganda...this has the effect of **deifying** data in the computer: the increasing use of the computer as a medium for storing data, and the mystique associated with its use, often

leads to the unconscious assumption that it possesses even more authority than was formerly accorded to the printed work.

Chandler's comments highlight both forks of our path with the same linguistic device of metaphor: the computer is cast simultaneously in the role of human and superhuman (it possesses authority, is god-like) and in the bodily extension role of storage container. At this point in the journey it is necessary to establish the power of metaphor in language usage and to demonstrate how thoroughly it has infiltrated and permeated computer discourse.

Metaphors that mesmerise

The illustration below shows what the sorcerer's apprentice can get up to when given the time and space to explore some of the rooms in the house of language. Whether this is a prison house (Jameson, 1972) of language is, of course, a fascinating issue which an examination of metaphor helps to clarify.

(Times Educational Supplement, 17 May 1991)

Metaphors are part of the magic, Orphic song of language because of their power to link concepts with each other in novel and surprising ways. The linkages thus created enable us to think about the abstract in concrete terms. The example above provokes the onlooker to conceive computers in terms of a postal transport system, 'delivering the goods'. It is easy to conjure this image up in the mind's eye, to connect it with that bulky parcel perched precariously on the doorstep, waiting to be unpacked. As part of our day-to-day language, metaphors function partly to construct meanings which are plausibly 'real' because they belong firmly to everyday experience. As Valerie Shepherd (1990) indicates, our culture talks about argument with frequent recourse to military metaphors ('attacking a weak point', 'shooting them down') because our culture views argument as adversarial, not co-operative. It would appear strange if we used the metaphor of dancing, 'taking our partners for the argument', to describe this aspect of behaviour. On the other hand, as she goes on to argue, our choice of metaphors can limit rather than liberate. I suggest that this happens because cultures evolve dominant metaphor linkages for their experiences, linkages which serve to suppress some meanings rather than others. In my example above, the cartoonist presents to the reader a conception of computing which is very familiar: metaphorically speaking, an efficient and effective Royal Mail 'special delivery' imbued with the positives of speed, unambiguity and clear sense of direction. However, the postal metaphor of delivery operates very differently if the linkage is made to delivery and childbirth. This experience is frequently slow, ambiguous and without a clear sense of direction. Hard-pressed teaching staff have, not infrequently, the same sort of experiences with keyboards and software yet the dominant metaphor hides this in favour of a positive postal delivery linkage. To paraphrase both Lakoff & Johnson and Valerie Shepherd, computers are to a large extent identifiable with 'the metaphors we live by'.

The thinking and assumptions which lie behind the metaphors can be made visible through analysis, criticism and reflection. These skills and activities are worthwhile educational practices, particularly in English and language teaching. The pervasive influence of a range of metaphors used to talk about the curriculum has been well illustrated by Keith Morrison (1989). He warns against the use of metaphors in the National Curriculum debate which 'risk suppressing...debate' and 'reduce the complexity of the curriculum to simplistic half truths' (p. 77). His analysis reveals a number of curriculum metaphors - delivery system, structure, machine and map - which in his view link the concept of the curriculum to the concepts of planning, control and industry.

Computer discourse, like curriculum discourse, is characterised by the use of metaphor and I will outline a taxonomy of computer metaphors presently. Michel Foucault (1980) understands 'discourse' to relate to the ideologies and ways of thinking embodied by words, seeing language not as a mirror or carrier of reality but in an important regard, constitutive of it. I was using a computer with a Year 8 class in English in 1989 when Foucault's notion of 'discourse' and the role of metaphor in language struck me as worth integrating into my teaching. At that time two possibilities presented themselves for further development. The first was to analyse the range of metaphors used in computer discourse with a view to planning schemes of work which would help students to become critically aware of language usage. The second was to consider how students might be encouraged to create new metaphors to express their experiences with computers. The first line of development has proved easier than the second. I have found, as the rest of this chapter shows, that 'the study of metaphors [collaboratively with pupils and students] is a very potent means of identifying the starting points, the areas of agreement and disagreement, and values and beliefs...the exposure of these starting points clarifies the terms of, and positions adopted...and crystallises the nature of the responses' (Morrison, 1989). Encouraging pupils and students to coin new metaphors for their experiences and understandings is equally valuable. Valerie Shepherd argues persuasively that 'new metaphors can create new meaning' (1990, p. 25) as does Penelope Karovsky in her recent (1989) article 'Educational Technology's Metaphor':

> One way of coping with change and articulating our understanding of the physical world and of our social reality is in metaphorical terms. New metaphors give us new ways to interpret our experiences, to perceive our lives and therefore our realities...If, as educational technologists, we find our prevailing metaphors limiting or irrelevant, we ought to search for new metaphors with which to frame our questions.   Karovsky (1989) p.163

This creative activity is less easy to promote, although some of the work completed recently by a Year 10 class I have been teaching did add some new metaphors to already existing clusters in a revealing manner. I will describe these lessons presently. The path we have been taking over the computer in education territory now leads upwards to a vantage point where I want to survey and analyse the clusters of metaphor faintly visible in the terrain below. Echoing upwards are the sounds of a teacher-pupil dialogue from 1989 Year 8 class.

Four metaphors - plus one

(A small group of three pupils and their teacher are using **TRAY**)

Teacher: What does this instruction mean, 'Post the disk into the disk drive'?

Andrew: It means put it in the slot gently, carefully so you don't break it.

Teacher: What do you think of when you see the word 'command'?

Lorraine: You have to wind it up like a toy, otherwise it doesn't work.

The figurative language in this brief dialogue embraces metaphor and simile drawn from the discourses of transport, the military and the machine. Two of these, **transport** and the **military**, will emerge presently as significant metaphor clusters in computer discourse. Andrew was asked why he thought the user manual had the verb 'post' instead of simply 'put': he replied that 'post' meant putting something carefully and deliberately in the post-box so it was not damaged and got torn up during its journey. Lorraine agreed, saying that 'command' had to be a 'strong word' otherwise people would 'do what they liked' with the computer. The focus on, and prompting about this particular choice of words has already started both Andrew and Lorraine on a critically aware examination of vocabulary resonances.

Advertisements for computer hardware and software are a rich source of metaphor in addition to user manuals and reviews in the press. Here are some examples which belong to a further three metaphor clusters:

(1)
QUIZ No 1
CAN YOU SPOT
THE ODD ONE OUT?
**Hardware Software Wear and Tear
Footware Tupperware**

(2)
LET YOUR FINGERS DO THE WALKING......
INFORMATION HANDLING IN A WINDOWS ENVIRONMENT

(3)
Extraordinary what you can grow from an Acorn

The Advertising Agency working for Toshiba in (1) has spotted an effective word-play on 'ware/wear' and emphasises, through repetition, the **merchandise** and 'goods for sale' origin in the Middle English **ware**. The copy for Oriel database and graphic display utilities in (2) presents the word 'windows', which belongs to a familiar **household** metaphor cluster. Finally, the third advertisement for Acorn computers identifies learning development with the growth of an oak tree, an example of frequent **organic** metaphors. An analysis of advertisements, user manuals and press copy reveals five major metaphor clusters: **transport, military, merchandise, household, organic.** Listed here are some examples from each cluster:

TRANSPORT	MILITARY	MERCHANDISE	HOUSEHOLD	ORGANIC
post	capture	aftermarket	architecture	acorn
delivery system	crash	appliance computer	breadboard	apple
address bus	control	audit trail	bug	apricot
buffer	command	software	byte	dedicated
chassis	deadlock	hardware	nybble	demented
mailbox	escape	firmware	menu	fatherfile
portability	break	vapourware	garbage	interface
track	save	wetware	housekeeping	icons
load	lock	liveware	nesting	earcons
pipe	monitor	package	mouse	virus
hotline			window	vaccine

It is with some justice that Michael Heim could claim in his essay on language processors in *The State of the Language* (1990) 'During the 1980s a new vocabulary established the computerisation of English...You learned to speak of files having no apparent physical dimension, **menus** offering a selection of non-edibles, and **monitors** providing vigilance over your own words'. The power of metaphor to spotlight selected aspects of a reality but also to obscure others is illustrated in Heim's examples of files which are not made of paper and menus which do not list protein. In the same vein a recent *Times Education Supplement* (17 May 1991) previewed 'Tutor treasures: a new crop from Apple' while an article on the computer page in *The Guardian* (14 March 1991) advised readers on the subject of 'Avoiding the mouse trap - pointers to the future'.

This language of computer discourse functions to create a double hazard for the unwary, but simultaneously to offer teaching and learning opportunities. The first hazard lies in the prevalence of metaphor itself, whereby there is a danger for us, as teachers and pupils, of confusing literal reality (our actual computer-based experiences) with analogy reality (metaphors). This is particularly so as we go 'cutting through an undergrowth of advertising hype, media fictions and commercial propaganda' to repeat Theodore Roszak's phrase (Roszak, 1986, p. xi). A stern warning from Craig Brod's *TechnoStress: the Human Cost of the Computer Revolution* (1984) alerted readers to the seductive power of word-processing software with names like *Magic Pen* and *Easy Writer*. This metaphoric analogy reality has the capacity to create 'sky high expectations' whereas actual empirical experiences frequently bring us down to earth on a steep 'learning curve' (1984, p. 131). The second hazard becomes visible once we look at the pattern and distribution of the five metaphor clusters: **transport, military, merchandise, household, organic**. To take up the trail again of this path through the computer in education territory we find ourselves back at the fork: three of the metaphor clusters offer us the computer as rule-governed machine: **transport, military, merchandise**. Yet, to quote Tibor Vamos (1987, p. 353) 'Human life is not a binary system... future society should not be a disciplined, well-ordered army'. The other two metaphor clusters, **household** and **organic** promise us technology we can identify with, feel comfortable with, almost speak the same language. The line between mind and machine shifts as the discourse works in us and upon us. The winds of change seem to be blowing in opposite directions at once.

An education goal for teachers of English working with language is to offer pupils and students opportunities for examining whether computer discourse is a prison house of language or not. The next section of this chapter describes a scheme of work taught during one week with a class of Year 10 students and makes some reference to National Curriculum areas and issues.

Classroom encounters of the fourth year kind

I planned three 50-minute lessons with a Year 10 class during March 1991 with the twin aim of (a) developing their awareness of how metaphor works in computer discourse and (b) giving them opportunities to work with language in order to respond critically to the issue of the computer's place in society. The writing outcomes were intended to form part of their GCSE coursework and the discussion points part of oral assessment opportunities in subsequent weeks. The planning took into account particular Statements of Attainment in Attainment Targets 2 (Reading) and 3 (Writing) together with detailed provisions in the Programmes of Study (POS) for Listening, Speaking, Reading and Writing. Here are relevant curriculum references from *English in the National Curriculum: No.2* (DES, March 1990):

AT2 Level 6: show in discussion of their reading an awareness that words can change in use and meaning over time. Example: Understand that technological developments, euphemism...contribute to language change (p.9).

AT2 Level 7: show in discussion or in writing an awareness of...literary devices and the effect on the reader.. Example: metaphors, personification (p.10).

AT2 Level 9: show in discussion and in writing an ability to recognise techniques and conventions of presentation in non-literary and media texts, and judge the effectiveness of their use (p.11).

In the POS documentation the following provisions are explicit:

Activities designed to develop pupils' knowledge about language should encourage discussion of vocabulary which is specific to:

- certain occupations e.g the specialist terms and acronyms used by groups such as...computer experts (p.26).

...the use of information technology might furnish...topics for discussion for which planned outcomes, **e.g. in written work or presentation**, might emerge (p.26).

Pupils should discuss:

- new words that have become part of the English vocabulary during the last 50 years or so **e.g. computer.**

- the reasons why vocabulary changes over time **e.g....the effects of advertising...new inventions and technology** (p.32-3).

Our first lesson began with an introductory phase in which some individual jottings of all the computer names the class could remember was followed by an instruction by me to 'group these names so that each group has something in common'. The results were intriguing as one example of this activity (Figure 1) shows.

Alphabetical groupings are complemented by a grouping which sees that some computer names are metaphors drawn from fruits which 'grow on trees'. We discussed other groupings: 'Nimbus' and 'Archimedes' were grouped together because it was felt they had a Latin and Greek tone of 'authority'. This was followed by an around-the-class question and answer exercise: 'How is a ball like an echo?' 'Why is the expression "a thorn in the flesh" like "marking a player out of the game?"' This phase on working with examples of metaphor led to the class copying down some metaphor slogans from television advertisements: 'Direct debit makes bills easier to swallow' and 'The spring collection from Woolworth's' and deciding whether they were effective or not. This phase, which ended this lesson, made clear the deliberate use of metaphor to promote one meaning (the television images of children cheerfully bouncing up and down for Woolworth's 'Spring' clothes collection; an easy way of paying bills) but also to suppress another (prices can spring upwards, too; bills are always bad for the digestion).

Our second lesson began by noting down a brief definition of metaphor - 'understanding one thing in terms of another' - and recapping what was now obvious: metaphors are chosen deliberately to create particular effects. The grouping of computer names 'Acorn' 'Apple' 'Apricot' was introduced again and an examination of the advertising copy-line 'Extraordinary what you can grow from an Acorn' undertaken.

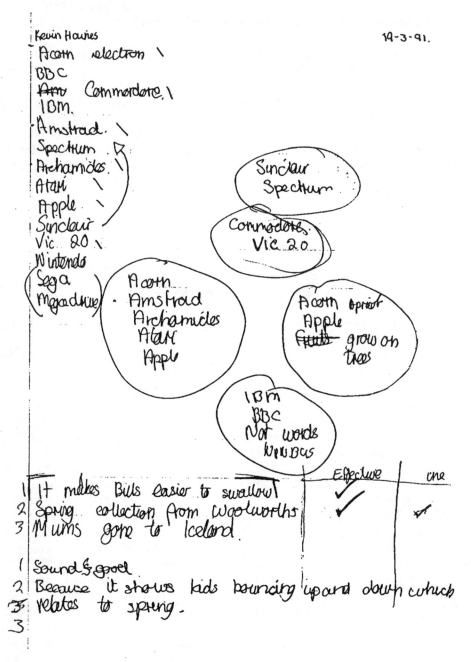

Kevin Havies   19-3-91.
Acorn   electron \
BBC
~~Ata~~   Commordore. \
IBM.
Amstrad. \
Spectrum ↘
Archamides. \
Atari   \
Apple   \
Sinclair ⟋
Vic 20 \
Nintendo
Sega
Megadrive

Sinclair
Spectrum

Commodore.
Vic 20

Acorn
• Amstrad
Archamides
Atari
Apple

Acorn apricot
Apple
~~Fruit~~ grow on
trees

IBM
BBC
Not words
Wews Bus

1 It makes Bills easier to swallow   Effective   one
2 Spring collection from Woolworths   ✓   ✓
3 Mums gone to Iceland.

1 Sound & ~~good~~
2 Because it shows kids bouncing up and down which
3 relates to spring.
3

Fig. 1.

Scepticism crept in: it takes months and years for an acorn to grow into a sturdy, reliable oak just as it takes months and years for tables and spellings to be learned. Can using a computer guarantee the same results in an electronic instant? Perhaps the metaphor is engaging in some sleight of hand?In the next phase the class worked in groups of three or four. Each group had lists of word-processor commands drawn from different software such as *View, Wordstar, Interword.* Their task was to compare the workings of a kitchen food-processor with the workings of a word-processor by finding word-processor commands that matched food-processor operations. A food-processor processes food, a word-processor processes words.

Here are some results:

FOOD-PROCESSOR	WORD-PROCESSOR
chop	cut and paste
knead	
mix	block text
blend	reform text, format text
beat	
whip	
grate	tab
slice	delete margin

The purpose of this task was to encourage the class to think in metaphors in preparation for an advertisement-based activity in part of the third lesson.

This final lesson of the week was divided into two parts with a range of writing options set for homework. I briefly reviewed some of the food/word-processor suggestions made during the previous lesson and then dictated 5 groups of 4 words each, also writing them on the board in 5 columns. These words e.g. 'post', 'capture', 'hardware', 'mouse', 'virus' were drawn from the five metaphor groups **transport; military; merchandise; household; organic** which have been discussed previously in this chapter. I told the class that all these words were used in computer manuals or advertisements and asked them to think of a heading or title which would describe each group. The class, working in pairs, offered this variety.

[TRANSPORT]:   ROYAL MAIL SORTING OFFICE

[MILITARY]:   ARMY PRISON, PRISONER-OF-WAR CAMP

[MERCHANDISE]:   TRADING, COMMERCE

[HOUSEHOLD]:   CAFE, DOMESTIC, RESTAURANT

[ORGANIC]:   HOSPITAL, GENETIC

It was clear, then, that all of us had interpreted the metaphors along roughly the same lines. We then discussed some of the ideas behind each group, e.g. delivery, control, domesticity.

The second part of the lesson was again pairwork in which I gave each pair an advertisement presenting a particular make of computer or computer system. The task now was to read the words and study the visuals in the advertisement carefully with the aim of picking out any metaphors and being ready to comment on them. This analysis was carried out and then pairs explained what lay behind the metaphors they spotted: 'EVERYONE DESERVES A CLASSICAL EDUCATION' took us back to the notion of 'authority' and the names 'Archimedes' and 'Nimbus', for example.

At the end of the lesson I gave each student a sheet with this variety of writing tasks to choose from for homework:

CHOOSE ONE WRITING TASK: ABOUT 300 WORDS

1. Your local doctor's surgery has just decided to offer a computer diagnosis service for patients. Design a leaflet which will both inform and encourage patients to use the service.

2. 'Legal decisions should be made by computer'. Do you agree?

3. Choose one advertisement for computers. Write a letter to the Plain English Campaign showing why the language is over-complicated, misleading or otherwise unsatisfactory.

    Plain English Campaign
    Vernon House
    Whaley Bridge
    Stockport
    SK12 7HP

4. Design an advertisement for a powerful new computer which has just come on the market. Use as many METAPHORS as possible.

My evaluation of the classroom-based lessons was that the class had developed their awareness of how metaphors work in computer discourse. The homework was designed to present further opportunities to explore metaphor but also to stimulate their responses to the question of the role of technology in society. I was particularly interested in the vocabulary, structures and presentation of their own language in these writings. The choices made by the 27 students were distributed into 15 responses on the legal decision essay type question, 8 who designed advertisements, 3 who designed doctor's surgery leaflets and just one letter to the Plain English Campaign.

What came out strongly across this range of writings was the students' ingenuity and sensitivity in constructing persuasive text, either discursively or creatively, and the awareness of technology's limitations. There were many examples of figurative language, including metaphors expected and unexpected. The student who wrote to the Plain English Campaign was forthright in stating 'Many metaphors are used to exaggerate points and advertising is a prime example of this'. The doctor's surgery leaflets sometimes combined word-processing text with graphics or line drawing and produced fertile metaphors for example 'The system relies on a powerful IBM computer, which operates the new programme called FRIENDS (Fast, Reliable, Internal Electronic Diagnosis System)' and 'This excellent service offers you professional medical advice, using the "Doctor Bytes Medical Advice Programme" operated on the Surgical PC computer'. The computer advertisements produced a range of metaphors, some of which were novel members of the clusters presented earlier in this chapter and discussed in class lessons:

TRANSPORT: speed of delivery was frequently emphasised e.g. 'The Dedrad QV has lightning responses and loads in an instant'; '...you can't see it for dust as it leaves the other machines in the mire' (mixed!); '...enabling you to word process all your business items in a flash'; 'faster than a speeding bullet'.

ORGANIC: the idea of superhuman figured here in addition to notions of authority e.g. '...the KING of the computers'; 'The brand new GENIUS 5000'; '...no more slaving for hours waiting for your files to load'; '...has whisper quiet operation'; 'Even our software is known as the "Cream of the Crop" for quality'; '...that's an IQ of 7000'.

The commentaries on legal and medical computer decisions and diagnosis were generally critical and discriminating. Many advantages and disadvantages of technology use were cited, showing that many students were clearly alert to the empowering and imprisoning features of computer discourse. Here are some examples:

'How would computers know what sentence a guilty person should get? It varies in different cases and can be affected by many different things.
Speeding is also very complicated and decisions made concerning fines and bans vary according to circumstances and conditions'.

'This is wrong as in some cases the computer wouldn't take things into account like...madness, epilepsy, jealousy...to take that into account you would have to be human'.

'Surely they are wrong, for the computer programs would have the programmer's view and bias, and therefore it doesn't remove the human traits not wanted'.

'No computer has yet been made with an empathetic feeling that would take into account the client's financial situation, health, mental disposition, responsibilities, employment and debts'.

'Another legal decision a computer could make in court is that some judges are corrupted and accept money to keep someone out of prison. A computer would not accept bribes...'

'The machine does not print prescriptions, your doctor is only authorised to do this'.

This scheme of work, which was only three periods long, left me quite satisfied. Not only the writings that came out of them but also the enquiring and freshly curious reactions of the students to the activities on metaphor showed it was worthwhile. Whether or not, to quote Terry Eagleton '...there is more metaphor in Manchester than there is in Marvell' (1983, p.6), our class certainly found this study of computer discourse a motivating experience.

> The Atoms of Democritus
> And Newton's Particles of light
> Are sands upon the Red sea shore
> Where Israel's tents do shine so bright
> (William Blake 1757-1827)

William Blake's generation developed a wave of technologies following Newton's discoveries in gravitation and optical physics. If your theoretical model of the universe was based on a particle metaphor, thought Blake, then you ran the risk of turning it into dust. Far better, therefore, to exchange this particle metaphor for a spiritual one in order to retain contact with life created by God and not mankind. Blake's concern with technology, language and metaphor is remote only in terms of time from the concerns of this chapter. I began with Dickens' *Little Dorrit* and a glance sideways at the orange Apricot brand name metaphor on my computer. I end it with a further glance sideways at the caption over a photograph of a mini-computer: 'Expertise injected by computer', (*Times Higher Educational Supplement*, 14 June 1991). This caption begins a feature on a hand-held computer capable of calculating correct insulin doses for diabetic sufferers. My fourth year students would be interested in this after their work on computer-based medical diagnosis and the role of metaphor in computer discourse. When Neil Postman wrote: 'And our languages are our media. Our media are our metaphors. Our metaphors create the content of our culture', (1987, p.15) he joined a lineage in which William Blake and all of today's pupils, students and teachers of English have a legitimate educational interest.

Acknowledgement

I am grateful to Sue and Jane Shaw and students at the Bishop Luffa School and Chichester High School for Boys, Chichester for their help and co-operation.

References

Brod, C. (1984) *TechnoStress: the Human Cost of the Computer Revolution*. New York.

Chandler, D. (1990) The Educational Ideology of the Computer. *British Journal of Educational Technology*, 21(3) pp. 165-174.

DES (March 1990) *English in the National Curriculum* , No. 2. London: HMSO.

Eagleton, T. (1983) *Literary Theory*. Oxford: Blackwell.

Foucault, M. (1980) in Gordon, C. (ed.), *Power-Knowledge: Selected Interviews and other Writings 1972-1977*. Brighton: Harvester.

Heim, M. (1990) Infomania, in Ricks, C. & Michaels, L. (eds.), *The State of the Language*. London: Faber.

Ihde, D. A. (1975) A Phenomenology of Man-Machine Relations, in Feinberg, R. & Rosemont, E. (eds.) *Work, Technology and Education*. Urbana, Illinois: University of Illinois Press.

Jameson, F. (1972) *The Prison-House of Language*. New York: Princeton University Press.

Karovsky, P. (1989) Educational Technology's Metaphors. *British Journal of Educational Technology*. 20(3) pp. 157-163.

Lakoff, G. & Johnson, M. (1980) *Metaphors We Live By*. Chicago: University of Chicago Press.

Morrison, K. (1989) Curriculum Metaphors and Control: the Old and the New. *Curriculum* 10(2) pp. 171-183.

McLuhan, M. (1964) *Understanding Media: The Extensions of Man*. New York: The New American Library.

Postman, N. (1985) *Amusing Ourselves to Death*. London: Methuen.

Roszak, T. (1986) *The Cult of Information*. New York: Pantheon Books.

Shepherd, V. (1990) *Language Variety and the Art of Everyday*. London: Pinter.

Vamos, T. (1987) Education and Computers: the Human Priority. *Prospects*, 17(3) pp. 349-353.

Wolfe, T. (1968) 'Suppose he is what he sounds like...', in Stern, G. E. (ed.) *McLuhan Hot and Cool*. London: Penguin.

10
Postwriting software and the classroom

Noel Williams

What is postwriting software?

We can view writing as a three-stage process of prewriting, composing and postwriting. Prewriting consists of activities such as planning, getting ideas and gathering information. Composing is the main business of getting words onto the page. Postwriting consists of activities such as revision, proof-reading, editing, checking for errors and infelicities. Typically postwriting occurs when a draft has been produced, and leads to a final draft, a publication.

However, it would be wrong to assume that a writer engages in these sets of processes in a strictly linear order (as the sequence: 'plan - draft - revise' suggests). Writers move from one process to another in ways which are meaningful to them. Some may operate quite strictly, not writing a word of draft until the plan is complete, not evaluating the draft until it is finished. Others may move apparently randomly from planning to drafting to re-planning to revising to drafting to planning again, flitting between various sub-processes as particular desires or ideas arise.

Postwriting computer systems are those such as spelling checkers, which aim to improve a text which has been produced. This may be a 'final draft', an interim draft, or even a fragmentary piece of text at some stage before incorporation into a draft. Whatever the status of the text, a postwriting analysis assumes that it is intended as finished text. Such computer systems therefore aim to validate what has been written, to ensure that it is correct or appropriate, and to advise on ways of improving the text.

Their validity within the writing process depends to some extent on the status of the draft being analysed. The less finished the text, the less valid the judgement of postwriting software. However, used sensitively, postwriting tools can support writing at any stage within the whole process.

In this paper I shall briefly describe a few of the most significant postwriting systems, and then evaluate their functions both generally and in terms of the classroom. To date, little postwriting software has been produced for education in the UK, but much has been used in the USA. After describing the main features of postwriting software, I shall identify some of their attractions and drawbacks and briefly consider how they might be usefully developed for schools.

Current postwriting systems

Most commercial postwriting software aims to check spelling, style or grammar. It is usually written for microcomputers, generally the IBM PC or clones, as the developers see the primary market as business report writing, not education. Spelling checkers are well known, compatible with most word processors and available for most microcomputers, so I shall devote little time to them. Style checkers and grammar checkers, however, are less well known. Some of the most well-known commercially available systems are *Grammatik IV* (apparently about to be updated as *Grammatik V*), *PC Style* (now called *PC Stylist*), *Readability*, *Corporate Voice*, *Rightwriter*, *Macproof*, *Stylewriter* and *Writer's Workbench* (for some of these see Rightwriter 1985; Grammatik 1990; Scandinavian PC Systems 1988, 1990; Seiter 1989). Two other systems which I shall refer to, *Critique* and *Ruskin*, are not generally available, but are research systems which give insight into what is possible and what the limitations of postwriting are. Most of the systems listed here overlap in functions, some offering more and others less. However, it is not always clear what a system offers, nor what its limitations are. Part of my aim here is to give some guidance in judging such systems.

Postwriting functions

1. Readability

The simplest critique most generally available is readability analysis, because it is simple to write computer programs which carry out such analyses (see for example Williams 1983, 1988b). The most well known of these is Gunning's Fog index, but many others exist. Those of Flesch, of Kincaid and Coleman-Liau are quite commonly used (Flesch 1948; Kincaid & Delionbach, 1973; Coleman & Liau, 1975). All are similar in attempting to grade the difficulty of a text (its readability) using a simple numeric formula. The formula is usually a function of average word length and average sentence length, which may be measured in a variety of ways. Application of a readability formula to a text results in a number which can be read off a table (in the case of the Fog index) or correlated with reading age or, in the case of US readability, grade level.

2. Pattern matching

The phrase 'pattern matching' covers a wide range of computer operations. After readability, it is the next simplest class of programs to write, so the next most common found in postwriting programs. A pattern is usually a string of characters (for example a sequence of letters representing a word), but more sophisticated systems will match patterns which include some variation in the string, and patterns of syntactic classes rather than simply character or word forms.

A spelling checker matches word patterns, for example. The simplest spelling checker holds a list of all the allowed word forms in a language, compares each word form in the text with its list, and if there is no match, reports an error. More sophisticated spelling checkers construct allowable words from basic word-parts (such as prefixes and suffixes added to a root form) according to the rules of English (or any other language) and test words in a text against those constructs. Both approaches may fail to recognise legitimate words (if they are rare, for example).

The sophisticated approach, though more 'natural' may also accept words which are unacceptable (for example **lionness** for **lioness**, based on a rule of root noun plus **-ness**) and neither takes any account of context. So the sentence **Her principle feet was to practice as a made** would be perfectly acceptable to almost all spelling checkers. Some are now being developed with a little syntactic information, so might recognise **practice** and **made** as errors, but even syntactic information cannot recognise the error of **feet** for **feat**.

Other patterns easily recognised by computer include acronyms (described to the computer as sequences of capital letters, so capitalised headings can be erroneously flagged), simple syntactic patterns which are signalled by word forms, such as split infinitives (described as the pattern **to + any word + a verb infinitive form**, and fooled sometimes by prepositional phrases such as **to every train** in **messages were sent to every train**) and abbreviations (a pattern described as: 'a word followed by a full stop which is not followed by a word whose first letter is capitalised').

Such information can be useful in editing and proof-reading, but is usually of limited value to the average writer.

3. Grammar

More sophisticated pattern matching identifies grammatical categories, using a parser of some kind. A parser is simply a computer program that acts as pupils learning traditional grammar used to working through a sentence and assigning a grammatical category to each word in the sentence.

This may be done probabilistically (Cherry 1978; McMahon *et al.*, 1978), using such rules of thumb as 'if the word before was an article, then the current word is probably a noun or an adjective'. Probabilistic parsers need only a very small dictionary of word forms to carry out their analysis, which is computationally attractive as it saves memory, but probabilistic parsers are easily confused by slightly unusual text, such as an ungrammatical essay or a creative short story.

More accurate parsers need dictionaries of the entire language, annotated for syntactic class. Such dictionaries can be very large and compiling them is expensive, so few postwriting systems incorporate them. They also can be slow (in computer terms, that is) and still make errors. The so-called 'garden path' sentence is beyond the wit of almost all current parsing designs. A garden path sentence is one which appears to have one syntactic structure, so leads the reader up the garden path of one interpretation, but then turns out really to have a different structure, which means the reader has to go back and re-interpret it, as in **The sausage rolls on the**

baker's shelf and hits the pastry. Most people (and most parsers) reading this sentence first understand **rolls** as a plural noun, with **sausage** as an adjective modifying it. When the reader encounters **hits** the sentence seems to be wrongly constructed, so the reader goes back and recognises **rolls** as a verb, with **sausage** as its subject noun. Computers have great difficulty with such constructions.

A full parse of a sentence yields all sorts of complex syntactic information. No postwriting system indulges in a full parse. Only IBM's *Critique*, which remains a research system after nearly ten years research (Miller, 1980, 1985; Miller et *al.*, 1981; Heidorn et *al.*, 1982; Richardson, 1985) approaches such analysis. All others content themselves with small descriptions. Usually they list the word classes found, giving a percentage of each (which most writers are not competent to interpret) and identify occurrences of certain patterns which can be predicted from word class information with reasonable confidence, such as the number of passive sentences, the distribution of different sentence openers and the occurrence of split infinitives. More complex (but more useful) information such as failure of agreement between subject and verb, or the distance between subject and verb are sometimes also offered, but not always reliably. *Ruskin*, for example, (Williams, 1988, 1989; Williams, et *al.*, 1988) offers both measures but, as it uses a probabilistic parser, makes errors as much as 25% of the time, which is unacceptably high for most users and almost worthless in the classroom, where the student has to believe that the computer has produced worthwhile feedback.

4. Indices of style

Alongside grammatical information, the so called stylecheckers provide various indices of style. 'Style' is used by the marketers of postwriting systems to mean just about any feature of writing that a computer can find some information on. It does not, therefore, involve assessment of 'tone', 'mood', 'nuance', 'persuasiveness', 'affect' - or a hundred other qualities we might use in characterising the style of a text. Largely style information records systematic variation in text which may, or may not, be significant stylistically.

As with the other postwriting information, style indices vary in availability largely as a function of ease of design. As a general rule, the less useful a piece of 'style' information is to a writer, the easier it is to implement and therefore the more frequently will you find it in postwriting systems!

So lists of different word and phrase types are easy to provide as they use the same kind of word-based pattern matching found in spelling checkers. Many postwriting systems therefore can identify long lists of jargon, abstract words and different vocabulary types (such as sexist words, informal language, colloquial words, persuasive words). *Grammatik IV* is probably the most comprehensive system in this respect, and also offers quite sensitive accounts of many of the items it lists.

Style analysis may also use rather debatable judgements such as the 'strength' of a text (based on lists of 'strong' words), or its 'negativeness', based on lists of negative words. *Rightwriter* is one system which judges 'strength' based on word lists.

The other indices computers can easily find are those of length. Figures for average word length, sentence length and paragraph length can easily be offered by computers. Similarly systems can identify all words, sentences or paragraphs which are unusually long. 'Unusual' may be defined by the system according to a pre-programmed norm, may be set by the user as a threshold length she or he wants to watch out for, or can be determined statistically (for example by identifying all sentences whose length is two standard deviations greater than the mean length of sentences in the text).

5. Frequency of items

Computers are good at counting. Anything they can find in the above list of information can also be counted. Postwriting systems offer counts of anything from 'abstractness' (for example *Writer's Workbench* is based on 1960s psychological research on the relative abstractness of words) to 'persuasiveness' as in those systems based on the use of modal verbs, 'strong' words and lack of negatives.

Postwriting systems can also provide counts of 'topics'. In fact these are usually counts of word tokens (so that, for example, **sing, sings, singing** and **sang** would all be counted as different words, hence different topics). However, the user can look for groups within such topic lists and therefore perhaps identify overused words or under-stressed topics.

6. Comparison with ideals

Most useful definitions of style relate a text to a norm of some kind, either by reference to previous texts in that style, or to some normative influence in the external context. So it can be useful to compare the computer's assessment of a text with other texts which 'define' the target style or to some description of the norms in the context of writing.

Writer's Workbench approaches this task by providing a 'style table' which is a statistically derived model of 20 texts. The texts used for this model can be any set selected by the user, though they have to be fed into the computer and analysed before the table can be compiled. So a teacher might choose the 20 best essays on a given topic to create a style table for future writers on that topic, or 20 of D. H. Lawrence's short stories as a model for short story writers.

The information in the style table is, of course, only that which *Writer's Workbench* is equipped to provide, so may ignore crucial indicators of the target style and may include indicators which are, in fact, irrelevant. Nevertheless, once such tables are compiled learners can compare their texts against any or all of the models and see how they match or fail to match in terms of the variables *Writer's Workbench* finds meaningful.

Corporate Voice and *Readability* (two related systems from Scandinavian PC Systems 1988, 1990) approach the problem in a similar way. However, their model of style is simpler than *Writer's Workbench*'s and presented in a more user-friendly fashion. These programs compile a graph of sentence length and word length for each sentence in the text. The graph is a 'scattergram', i.e. dots are 'scattered' across the graph, a dot being placed at each position on the graph for each sentence showing where the sentence length and average word length intersect.

Once the scattergram is drawn for a text, graphs of other styles can be superimposed upon it, so that sentences which fall outside the norm ('outliers') can be easily seen. Different styles can be selected from a simple menu, so the user can see quickly and easily which style his or her text most readily accords with.

The attractiveness of the *Corporate Voice* and *Readability* interface hides its substantial drawback. The very sophistication of the presentation suggests that the comparison is a significant one. By placing an ideal scattergram over that of the analysed text, the suggestion is that removing the outliers, making the two scattergrams fit, will make the styles the same and the texts of equal value. This, of course, is nonsense if the only grounds for the comparison are word and sentence length. It is also of little value if the intended style is not defined in the context the writer is aiming at. For example, if the style is 'journalism' are we comparing with *The Times'* leader, the *Guardian's* computer page or *The Sunday Sport*?

The only system which aims for a detailed description of the context of writing is *Ruskin*, a system developed at Sheffield City Polytechnic by CIRG. I have described the working of *Ruskin* in several papers (for example Williams 1988a, 1989) so will not repeat that description here. What *Ruskin* aims to do is allow the user to specify the context of writing, then compare the writer's text with its idea of all the variables in that context. This is a much more sophisticated idea than that used by any other postwriting system as it enables a very large range of different, particular contexts to be described by the user. However, as implemented, it is limited to a range of about fifteen variables meaningful for report writing, and the kinds of information *Ruskin* can match to context are still word length, sentence length, abstraction and so on - the kinds of information used by other stylecheckers.

7. Other features of analysis

Each postwriting system offers its own particular combination of analyses, and most have a unique feature of some kind. However, we have yet to see adventurous postwriting systems which trade on what is known of text organisation (for example the use of headings and text coherence) and presentation (for example the use of white space). Whilst sophisticated analysis of these areas would be beyond state of the art computing, **useful** analysis would not. For example, a system that examines the tags being used in a WYSIWYG (What You See Is What You Get) word-processor or a desk-top publishing system would be able to form quite valuable assessments of presentation. Computationally the kinds of analysis required are of the same order as those used in the other areas of postwriting analysis. As yet no system attempts to do this, but it is a logical development that will probably not be long in coming.

Evaluating postwriting software

It is probably clear from the above that postwriting systems can provide a large range of information, of variable quality, but that much of that information is unfocused. The system offers it but the writer or teacher must make of it whatever he or she wishes. As postwriting systems seldom focus on the kinds of information that teachers of writing see as most important (such as the organisation of the text, the logic of an argument, the creativity of the prose, the logic of sentences, the interest of the language, the use of other sources, the coherence of the text and so on), you might wonder if such systems have anything to offer in the classroom. I believe they do, if used sensitively and sensibly, but such use must be hedged with caveats. In particular, the teacher must take care to ensure that she or he knows **exactly** what it is that the computer system is providing. Relying on the manual is better than believing the marketing hype, but better still is to run the program on some difficult test cases, and even better is to understand the limits of the program that is carrying out the analysis.

Teachers often do not have the time to probe to such depths. So they must remember the general principle that the computer will not analyse the text as a person might, faced with the same task. The computer's analysis will be relatively mechanical, relatively inflexible and will always fail with some limiting cases of creativity or unusual text.

Herein, however, is one of the possible uses of the postwriting system in the classroom. The student can use the computer's analysis to compare with her or his own. Where the analysis disagrees, the student can strive to understand **why** there is a difference, i.e. what it is about the text which has made the computer reach its judgement, and what it is about his or her understanding of the text which shows the computer to be wrong. As a way of studying the different levels of language structure, the various kinds of ambiguity in writing, and the various kinds of context that can operate on interpretation, the computer can give all sorts of insight into the flexibility of the human language code because of the very inflexibility of its own.

The value of postwriting software

The models of writing used in postwriting software are often simpler than those the task actually demands. By and large no real analysis of the real problems of writers underlies postwriting software. The software design is driven by what can be implemented which **might** by of use to writers, rather than analysing the writer's need and then looking for computational solutions. Successful use of postwriting software in the classroom therefore depends on either a flexible attitude to the software (for example ignoring those parts of the system which do not match your writers' needs) or adapting your understanding of writing to fit the software's model. The latter approach is, of course, dangerous as there may be no real understanding of what goes on in writing within that software. Consequently it is often important to place postwriting tools in a **critical** classroom context, which encourages the learner to evaluate the software's judgement rather than simply accept it. In such a context inappropriate and erroneous judgement by the machine can be of real learning benefit as it encourages learners to defend their writing and to explore the variations in reaction and interpretation available to readers.

Whatever the teaching situation, choice (and use) of postwriting tools depends heavily on the functions those tools are intended to serve. If they are entirely for writers learning how to write, rather than supporting practising writers, postwriting systems can easily be approached critically and used in a wider learning environment which does not take the postwriting critique as gospel.

If, however, the emphasis is on supporting practising writers (for example by placing postwriting tools in a word-processing laboratory for students) then it will be inappropriate to set up a context in which the postwriting software is itself evaluated. A writer who is not primarily concerned with learning the craft wants computer tools which aid writing and improve its effectiveness without extra effort. Few writers will use computer tools if they make heavier demands on her or him than traditional writing tools.

As many learning contexts combine **both** these uses, teachers have to perform a balancing act, establishing the confidence of writers in the system(s) by enabling them to use those systems appropriately. For example, even a device as simple as a spelling checker must be understood if learners are not to believe that it will catch every error they make.

The needs of teachers and those of learners may also conflict. For example, a 'fast' system will be good for practising writers, should please learners, but may simply accumulate errors for the teacher to deal with. The output from style checkers is typically several pages, so if the learner needs tutor support in order to interpret that output (which is implied by a 'critical' context), the teacher may find that responsibility for mechanical correction is taken away but replaced by an overwhelming demand for detailed interpretative help.

Such interpretative support may well be needed in the typical classroom using postwriting, for the value of postwriting output depends both on the quality of the user interface and the nature of the hidden analyses that are actually carried out. It is hard for users to determine what programs actually do, and this may be disguised by an attractive interface (as in the *Readability* example above). The teacher needs to be sure of the validity of the software's observations (for example will it treat some prepositional phrases as if they were split infinitives, like **to every train**). The learner needs to be able to believe what the software offers if the teacher provides no interpretative context for it.

Worse than this, interfaces often simply provide numerical output, which of course needs further interpretation. Is a figure of 23% passive sentences good, bad or indifferent? At Sheffield, we have seen students receive numerical postwriting output and, given no guidance, simply decide that a particular number should be increased or decreased, so rewrite the text with the mechanical desire to 'decrease the number of passives' or 'reduce the length of eight sentences'. Such students have to be equipped with sufficient knowledge of language and perhaps of computing to be able to use, or ignore, such numbers.

Only in the simplest of writing training can the output from postwriting systems be allowed to stand. For example, adolescent writers getting to grips with reports for the first time have enough experience of language and a sufficiently simple task to find readability programs useful. If an adolescent novice report writer receives a poor readability grade, it is very likely that the student's sentences are too complex, the student has used too many tortuous expressions and the vocabulary can be simplified. This is a common set of flaws for such writers, and a computer can point it out just as easily as a human teacher.

Postwriting benefits

The benefits of postwriting software are not too difficult to enumerate. To begin with, 'mechanical' corrections of text need no longer be the learner's responsibility in some areas. Computers can assess **some** features of text as well as people, so teachers are freed to concentrate on higher order writing teaching. If the teacher can be confident of the program's algorithm and the likely relevance of its analysis, then he or she can sit back and allow the machine to apply its rules.

By sitting back the teacher can release more time for other purposes, whilst being sure that learners will gain a knowledge of writing which is detailed and **specific** to their text and, for some software, specific to their own situation. Analysis can also be carried out whilst other activities are performed, releasing both teacher and learner. Furthermore the software may well be more thorough and more comprehensive (in their limited analyses) than human assessors, for they suffer neither fatigue nor irritation.

The computer can also increase learners' motivation towards grammar and editing, just as computers by their novelty and attraction seem to increase motivation in many other areas. (However, for students who find computing a problem, postwriting systems will, of course, prove a further barrier to learning, not a motivator).

Learners typically spend more time over writing assignments when using computers to write and some report a lowering of stress, for feedback on their work can be private.

There are also possible spin-off benefits, as learners who only use computers for word processing can 'graduate' from that limited application to other functions of computers by perceiving the numerical, interpretative and graphical possibilities of postwriting systems. Some, for example, use postwriting tools to carry out simple stylistic analyses of text. *Grammatik IV* is useful for this as it allows users to define language patterns of their own interest and analyse text for those alone.

Possible drawbacks of postwriting in the classroom

As we have seen, postwriting software cannot assess semantics, pragmatics or discourse structure, and typically does not address presentation or organisation of text. In fact all of these could be addressed (in very narrow ways) by software, given the state of the art in natural language and artificial intelligence research, but there is unlikely to be any development in these areas without a shift in commercial or research preoccupations. So many of the most important characteristics of text remain unanalysed. For some teachers postwriting systems are a boon, as they find the computer takes care of the mechanics so they have more time for the substance. Others regret the use of postwriting tools, as it can deflect the learner's attention from issues of greater consequence.

Nor is postwriting software as sensitive to context as learners and teachers require, and it can be fooled by complex, clever or silly text. In a sense, postwriting tools are of most value to 'average' writers, if there are such beasts. The good writer will probably find that postwriting tools consume more time than they release. The poor writer is likely to be overwhelmed by the output, unable to deal with it without constant support, and as the software is typically not sensitive to the needs of poor learners it might be demoralising for them. Writers who hit the mean, making occasional errors and needing some guidance and those who have the capacity for improvement but need nudging in some directions will find that postwriting often enough hits the mark to be useful, but has not so much to say that they are swamped in depressing, uninterpretable output.

Undersupported learners may also over-correct or correct mechanically without understanding the reasons for the changes they make. They may concentrate on 'small' errors so miss grave ones and may need extra skills to cope with jargon or statistics in the output before they can apply them to their writing.

Finally there are flaws in postwriting software which are common to other classes of software:

- much postwriting software is not designed for the British educational context, so its relevance may be accidental;
- learners may need to develop extra skills to cope with computers in the first place (although this may, of course, be part of the intention of their use in the classroom);
- some software may be simplistic, prescriptive or make exaggerated claims (or all three of these!), so must be carefully evaluated.

Conclusion

Obviously postwriting software can be of use in the classroom and, with increasing sophistication, it may be increasingly useful. However, to be of wide and sustained value in UK education, more account must be taken of actual classroom needs and more sophistication is needed in the software itself, particularly in the areas of contextual flexibility and 'deep' analysis of text.

References

Cashdan, A., Holt, P. & Williams, N. (1986) *Report to the Manpower Services Commission on a Pilot Investigation into the Assessment of Written Style by Computer.* TEED, Moorfoot, Sheffield.

Cherry, L.L. (1978) PARTS - A System for Assigning Word Classes to English Text, *Computing Science Technical Report 81.* Bell Laboratories, Murray Hill, NJ 07974.

Coleman, M. & Liau, T.L. (1975) A Computer Readability Formula Designed for Machine Scoring, *Journal of Applied Psychology.* 60, pp. 283-284.

Flesch, R.F. (1948) A New Readability Yardstick. *Journal of Applied Psychology,* 32, pp. 221-233.

Grammatik (1990) Grammatik. *Mac User's Guide.* Reference Software International, San Francisco.

Heidorn, G.E., Jensen, K., Miller, L.A., Byrd, R.J. & Chodorow, M.S. (1982) The EPISTLE Text-Critiquing System. *IBM Systems Journal.* 21, 3, pp. 305-326.

Kincaid, J.P. and Delionbach, L.J. (1973) Validation of the Automated Readability Index. *Human Factors.* 15(1), pp. 17-20.

McMahon, L.E., Cherry, L.L. & Morris, R. (1978) Statistical Text Processing, *Bell System Technical Journal.* 57(6), July-Aug.

Miller, L.A. (1980) A System for the Automatic Analysis of Business Correspondence. *Proceedings of the First Annual National Conference on A.I.* Stanford University, pp. 280-282.

Miller, L.A., Heidorn, G. & Jensen, K. (1981) Text Critiquing with the Epistle System: An Author's Aid to Better Syntax *Proceedings of the National Computer Conference.* 50, pp. 649-655.

Miller, L.A. (1985) Computers for Composition: A Stage Model Approach to Helping. *IBM Research Report RC (#49957).*

Richardson, S.D. (1985) Enhanced Text Critiquing Using a Natural Language Parser. *IBM Research Report RC 11332 (#51041).* Box 218, Yorktown Heights, New York 10598

Rightwriter (1985) *Rightwriter, computer software.* RightSoft Inc.

Scandinavian PC Systems (1988) *Readability Program for the IBM PC, XT, and AT,* 2nd edn, Scandinavian PC Systems, PO Box 215, Uxbridge.

Scandinavian PC Systems (1990) *Corporate Voice, computer software.* Scandinavian PC Systems, PO Box 215, Uxbridge.

Seiter, C. (1989) Words, Words, Everywhere. *Macworld* October, pp. 22-36.

Williams, N. (1983) A Readability Index. *Practical Computing,* Dec, pp. 150-151.

Williams, N. (1988) Software for Writing Training, *Humanistiske Data,* 1, pp. 51-65.

Williams, N. (1988) Style Wars - Writing a PC Stylechecker. *Personal Computer World.* Jan.

Williams, N., Holt, P. and Cashdan, A. (1988) *Expert System for Report Writing, report to the Manpower Services Commission.* TEED, Moorfoot, Sheffield.

11
A story about storying

Harry McMahon and Bill O'Neill

Introduction

This is a story about storying. In telling our story we wish both to emphasise the primacy of storying to the human mind and to illustrate how we can exploit information technology without allowing it to distort our aims as educationalists interested in the development of literacy. Barbara Hardy (1977) cogently expresses the first point, 'My argument is that narrative, like lyric or dance is not to be regarded as an aesthetic invention used by artists to control, manipulate, and order experience, but as a primary act of mind transferred to art from life.' We wish to add that information technology, in the form of hypertext, hypermedia and multimedia, has the potential to mediate from life to art, allowing stories to be narrated through an integration of drawing, graphics, sound and non-linear text. While the technologies of pen and paper and the printing press bind the concrete manifestation of the story into a linear form, hypertext allows the links and connections made between aspects and elements of the story to be realised in an alternative, non-linear form, readily conceptualised by children. Our experience is that in telling stories through this medium children quickly develop the ability to create complex non-linear structuring.

Before continuing, a brief word about *HyperCard*, the software environment we have employed in our research: *HyperCard*, a software package launched over three years ago by Apple Computer, was first perceived by many, and indeed still is, as an environment for presenting information in the form of jazzed up databases incorporating graphics and sound. Many of the commercially available packages built on the *HyperCard* platform are of this type, databases of the artefacts held in a museum, or information on the adult education courses available in a city, or the properties for sale in a region. What is less widely recognised is that *HyperCard* has provided educators, and the children in their charge, with a rich environment in which text, graphics and sound can be related in the process of building knowledge, making meaning and communicating. When one sees the effects on language development of children beginning to experiment with the incorporation of sound into their storying and when it is recognised that their drawings no longer simply illustrate their story but have become integral aspects of the meaning-making process, one can see the power of the resources that are immediately available to children in *HyperCard*. When, for example, they are encouraged to communicate the personality of their characters through drawing, frequently highly complex personae, bubbling with character, are created. The challenge to the teacher is then to find ways to help children articulate these personae in text.

The critical reader will almost certainly experience feelings of déjà-vu; has this kind of thing not been said before about many other innovations? Why should *HyperCard* be any different? We support this critical perspective. For too long technology has been introduced into education for the wrong reasons. We are not making any claims about *HyperCard* as such. It is not the much sought after pre-packaged computer solution to educational problems, the 'ideal' program that teachers can buy off the shelf and bring into the classroom with the expectation that, if children are plugged into it, it will teach them what we want them to learn. The claims we are making relate to the creative use that teachers and children can make of this software environment in the classroom. In the tradition of good teaching, the use that we support for *HyperCard* is highly interactional, with pupils together collaborating with the teacher as they strive for shared understanding of an emerging world, encapsulated and represented for as long as it is educationally valuable to do so, in *HyperCard*.

Our first sentence in this chapter declared that we were intent upon telling a story about storying. Some stories begin at the beginning. This one did not. We have already declared our conclusions. Now it is time to begin the beginning.

The beginning

Around Christmas, 1988, co-author Harry McMahon, a weekend and holidays landscape artist, came upon something he had been seeking for a very long time, an affordable computer-based medium in which he could try combining his skills as an artist with those of computer-based learning developer. The acquisition of a Macintosh, with *HyperCard*, and sight of the graphical adventures of a Californian cat called Inigo, created by Amanda Goodenough, provided the stimulus to produce a graphical, animated adventure in which the heroine was Ginny, Harry's West Highland White Terrier.

Adults (teachers in particular) loved it; but it was not good enough for co-author Bill O'Neill, because in Bill's view it was not good enough for children. Ginny was Harry's dog and, even though her adventures took place in a recognisable local landscape, she still did not fully belong to the children. She was not already part of their world and that was what counted.

Harry's response to Bill's challenge was to provide Ginny with empty speech and think bubbles, as in a comic, inviting children to make her their own by having her, and other characters in the story, talk and think in the reader's own words. That way, Harry reasoned, ownership of the screen-based characters could be claimed by the children. As Harry saw it, it would not matter if the children could not yet type in what they wanted the characters in the story to say and think. The teacher could do that.

Fig. 1. Ginny encounters a crab on Portstewart Strand.

Fortuitously, fellow artist Orla, Bill's daughter, was also exploring *HyperCard* as an adventure story medium. Then seven years old, and for long a keen artist, she had become enthralled by this new medium. She quickly learned to use the graphics tools to draw characters, to place them in space by elaborating their background and to send them on adventures by linking cards in appropriate sequence. At just the same time as Harry was programming *HyperCard* to allow Ginny to talk and think, Bill noticed how Orla in her work in *HyperCard* was facing a difficulty commonly encountered by children when writing. One of her stories concerned Kim and Pat.

Although Orla had imbued her characters with much vitality - they were richly illustrated, oozing with personality and interest and owners of several Picassos, it seemed - her associated writing, in contrast, was rather pedestrian, simply relating a sequence of events. As Bill saw it, Orla was a specific case illustrating the generality that awareness of those aspects of language required for literacy does not develop spontaneously from spoken language. Faced by the task of writing rather than talking about Kim's and Pat's adventure, she was caught within a linear narrative form, unable to convey the richness of the knowledge of the characters she had created.

Fig. 2. Kim and Pat in the Picasso Gallery.

Bill's challenge as a parent, encountered at the same time as Harry was setting out to help children make Ginny speak and think, was then not only to cause Orla to recognise the need for elaboration and depth in her writing generally, but specifically to give her readers an insight into the two characters in her story.

Thankfully, and certainly not fortuitously, the critical recognition of the links between our separate explorations took place and the crucial step was taken. The ability to make characters speak and think was grafted into Orla's world - a world in which the characters already belonged to her. Kim and Pat were placed on a neutral (blank) background. Four icons, standing for access to thought and speech, were presented on the screen; pressing an icon allowed Orla to display, in a sequence under her control, a think or talk bubble for Kim or for Pat. Each successive bubble appeared empty of text, but with a flashing cursor inviting her to write. The technique exploited the 'natural' tendency of children to participate actively in dialogue - albeit in a highly stylised fashion.

Fig. 3. Kim and Pat in Bubble Dialogue.

When asked to explain what was happening between her two characters, Orla immediately responded, 'Kim and Pat love adventures. Pat loves motor bikes and Kim loves exploring'. Cohen & Manion (1985) define role play as 'participation in simulated social situations that are intended to throw light upon the role/rule contexts governing "real" life social episodes'. Orla had no difficulty taking up the opportunity to role play and had clearly defined the social episode. She almost instinctively pressed the 'say' icon for Kim so that she would be the first to be made to speak (predictably so, as almost all her toys are given female personae) and entered into the dialogue. Once Pat had been given his say, Bill (acting as typist and participant observer) asked Orla what Kim was thinking. A thoughtful pause - and the dialogue continued.

Fig. 4. Kim's private world is made public.

When Bill printed out the resultant text, reproduced below, Orla joyfully proclaimed that she had written a play. As in drama, this scripted text, whilst displaying many of the characteristics of written speech, now relies on the created context to set the scene.

Dialogue start: Orla's story:

[Kim and Pat love adventures. Pat loves motor bikes and Kim loves exploring.]

Kim says:	**Pat can we go exploring in that old cave near the river?**
Pat says:	**I wish that we could do something on motor bikes today.**
Kim thinks:	I wish we could find a dragon guarding some treasure.
Pat thinks:	I wish I could ride a motorbike.
Kim says:	**Why can't we go to the cave today and bikes tomorrow?**
Pat says:	**Sis why can't it be the other way around?**

Kim thinks:	Boys boys boys ! they are always a pain.
Pat thinks:	I wish Sis would stop getting my plans in a mess.
Kim says:	**Motor bikes are stupid. Why can't we go exploring for one day?**
Pat says:	**Well I think that exploring of yours is stupid too!**
Kim thinks:	Is there any way I can persuade him to go exploring?
Pat thinks:	Is there any way that I can persuade her to look at motor bikes?
Pat says:	**Why can't we forget all about this exploring of yours.**
Kim says:	**NO WAY.**
Kim thinks:	If we could go into the cave I wish my brother could get lost. And I'll never see him again.
Pat thinks:	When will Sis ever give in and let us see some motorbikes?
Pat says:	**I give in Sis we'll go to the cave today so long as we will see some motorbikes tomorrow.**
Kim says:	**YIPPY SKIPPY Let's go and pack our bags for the journey.**
Kim thinks:	I suppose boys aren't that bad after all.
Pat thinks:	Why did I ever give in.

Delighted with her play which she had imperceptibly created out of the dialogue, Orla wanted to act it out. Equally delighted with the outcome of this first use of what we later dubbed the 'Bubble Dialogue' tool, and the insight it gives on Orla's imaginative world and by extrapolation on her view of her social world, we set out to investigate if multimedia in general, *HyperCard* in particular, and within *HyperCard*, Bubble Dialogue and any other tools for literacy that might emerge, could be used to advantage by groups in classrooms.

Taking multimedia into the classroom

Children's stories, and it is storying that they do very well, are frequently scattered with the seeds of powerful imaginative ideas. One of the challenges for the teacher is to create frameworks which allow children to continue to sow these imaginative seeds but which also nurture their growth and development and their manifestation in literary form. Central to our thinking was that these supportive frameworks would be constructed by teacher and pupils working collaboratively. The computer might be brought to bear or used as a tool but it was the quality of the interaction between teacher and learners that would ensure quality learning.

It appeared to us, when we first contemplated taking digitised multimedia into classrooms, that *HyperCard* provided the central platform of a multimedia environment which would allow this interaction to take place and at the same time challenge learners to seek new and powerful means of expression. The multimedia environment consisted of a Macintosh computer with the *HyperCard* software and, in addition, a MacRecorder and scanner. The MacRecorder is a very easy but powerful sound digitiser which allows the learner to incorporate any sound from any source into their work. A scanner will digitise any photograph or drawing and thus allow them to be incorporated directly into the children's work on the computer. With these devices available in the classroom, all sound and graphics become an instant resource readily incorporated into children's work. The magic comes because children are operating with digitised sound, digitised graphics and digitised text; in this form, the sound, graphics and text all become fully manipulable, they can be cut and pasted, twisted, turned, repeated and linked in any number of ways. Thus in the *HyperCard* environment, for the first time ever, teachers could allow children's preferred medium to become central, allowing them, for example, to first tell their stories through drawing or music and only then elaborate them with text. Through this integration of and transference between media, children could be caused to reflect on the meaning-making process itself and on the contribution that text, sound/music and photographs/drawings/graphics can make to the process.

One cannot take technology into the classroom without the willing co-operation and full involvement of teachers, so our first steps were taken in collaboration with twelve teachers, drawn from one special, three primary and four secondary schools in Northern Ireland, rather than pupils. As we said at the beginning: storying is a fundamental human activity - it is difficult to imagine a classroom where stories are not the currency of communication. For this reason, in introducing teachers to this supposedly new world of multimedia, we constructed a storyboard, a framework for story writing, and set about engaging teachers in the creation of some collaborative stories. Having created a structure for their stories the teachers drafted them on a word-processor. It then proved a very simple step to move into *HyperCard*, where graphics and eventually sounds were added. The teachers moved from current good practice in the writing of stories to the creation of multimedia stories, from the known to the not so well known. Before long multimedia was seen by many of the teachers as a natural development of their own practice; they had been doing it all along. They were very quick to appreciate how the computer could empower their pupils, allowing them access to exciting new tools of expression and communication. They were equally quick to realise that this new environment would make major demands on them. While the vast majority immediately rose to the challenge and were rightly proud of their achievements at the end of the project, there were some frustrations along the way. Because, however, the teachers were an integral part of the project team, and although the setbacks were many - personal sickness, computers breaking down, software not working - as each new challenge was confronted their confidence in their own professionalism greatly increased. This was not a computer project, it was an educational one and they were the educationalists.

When the teachers moved the work into the classrooms the reactions of the children were even more exciting than we had anticipated. They responded with enthusiasm and imagination to the multimedia environment and made progress in the development of literacy that both delighted and startled the teachers. (A full report of this work has been submitted to the sponsoring body, the National Council for Educational Technology, and elements of the report will be published in due course.)

One of the characteristics of the work that was carried out over a two-year period was its diversity. Teachers were able to use the technology to foster the needs of their own pupils. In a sense, they created their own pedagogical solutions to the educational questions which arose in their classrooms. In the next section, we give a feeling of what was happening in several different schools by telling the story of what happened in one.

For two academic years, each of the five members of the Language Development and HyperMedia Research Group have worked in partnership with teachers in two of the schools described above. Bill's responsibilities included visiting a County Londonderry primary school on a regular basis, to work with the Primary 6 teacher, Seamus Coyle, who has contributed significantly to the development of the work of the research group. Stacy and Stephen emerged in Seamus' classroom.

Enter Stephen and Stacy

The process of collaborative story writing is never a simple one and even though one might attempt to document each stage of the process, the feeling often remains that only one aspect has been revealed, essentially because the dynamics of the relationships between the authors can remain opaque unless a great deal of attention is paid to it. Such is the case with the story of 'Stephen and Stacy', written by three less able 10 year olds, Kerry-Ann, Faye and Andrew. This brief account will have to gloss over much of the social dynamics which are critical to all collaborative episodes, and which added much richness to the process of writing this story.

The sequence of the story was simple but clear. On reading the first draft, Bill asked the children to explain their story using a comic-strip storyboard where the arrows represent the next act of the story, 'and then', indicating the transition from one scene to the next.

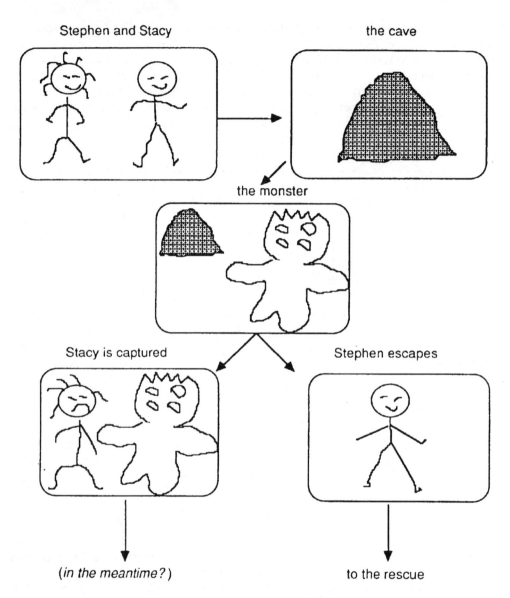

Fig. 5. The storyboard.

Not only did this simple technique allow the children to reflect on the structure of their writing, something with which many writers have difficulty, but it allowed them to contemplate the possibility of structural changes. Once the 'and then' links had been drawn, Bill suggested that, as our hero Stephen was off getting his Indiana Jones outfit so that he could come to the rescue, our heroine Stacy had to find a way to cope with the monster 'in the meantime'. Through the introduction of a new link in the story which allowed Stacy's account to be told, the possibility that Stacy could take control of her life was explored. In spite of the fact that two of the three members of the group were girls, there was resistance to this seemingly revolutionary idea. Perhaps because we had clearly pinpointed this issue in the comic-strip storyboard it continued to surface. The graphical representation of their story proved a good reference point as the story developed, helping the group to identify which aspects required elaboration.

One night at 8.30pm in Loughermore Forest above Ballykelly. Steven and Stacy went for a walk when all of a sudden Tracy saw a big creepy shadow beside a tree.

Fig. 6. Stephen and Stacey.

The children were introduced to *HyperCard* graphics and immediately proceeded to draw their characters: Stacy, Stephen and the Monster began to take form, but consistent with our previous experience with Bill's daughter Orla, while the children had imbued their characters with much vitality in the drawings, they were unable to convey the richness of the knowledge of the characters they had created. Thoroughly enjoying the power that *HyperCard* offered, the children created several screens and linked them together producing an action oriented comic strip of the rough outline, which they soon began to develop and expand upon.

At this stage of development in writing stories, much of children's writing is driven by the action of the story; 'and then', 'and then'....... Bubble Dialogue allowed us to pause the action without interfering with the flow of events. The ability to make characters speak and think was grafted into the children's world - a world in which the characters already belonged to them. The children's drawing of Stephen and Stacy was pasted into the Bubble Dialogue tool and the children invited to write what the two protagonists were thinking and saying.

Fig. 7. Bubble Dialogue: Stephen and Stacey.

This technique exploits the 'natural' tendency of children to actively participate in dialogue; focusing on the characters on the screen it draws on the interactional turn-taking aspect of conversation. By simulating the conversation situation, the Bubble Dialogue tool acts as a bridge from conversation to text, from talk through reflection to literacy, from embedded to disembedded language. It exploits the natural language of children, moving them easily and imperceptibly into the exploration of different aspects of language, from the informal language of the home and the playground to the more formal language of the school and on to the increasingly abstract language of written text.

As the children made Stacy and Stephen talk and think through the situation confronting them the characters slowly developed. Off screen, the children themselves became caught up in animated discussion as they increasingly identified with the characters, seeking to make them behave coherently within the context of the emerging story. Sometimes the children competed to control the characters. Most of the time they co-operated and co-created the public speech and private 'thoughts' of the characters on the screen. They were driven forward by the flow of events, by the turn-taking conversation-like scenario; but the pressure on the children to move on to describe the next thing that happened in the story, the next event, seemed to have eased as the characters were allowed to take their time to talk things out in context. The characters began to reveal their true selves, in what they were made to say, but more interestingly in what they were allowed to think but not to say. Right from the beginning, the children recognised the distinction between the private and the public world. Episodes in the dialogue such as Stephen's honest thought, 'I couldn't really save her but I wish I could impress her', indicate the children's ability to use the Bubble Dialogue tool to express their understanding of what should be private in a given social context.

In spite of such insights on the part of the children, the script emerging from the Bubble Dialogue reveals two rather shallow characters, somewhat staid and stereotypical, lacking subtlety. On completion of the dialogue the children, having switched into review mode, were able to start at the beginning of the story and amend the dialogue or add to it as required. In review mode, as well as having the dialogue already created visible and accessible to change, an empty text field becomes available in which the children can narrate the story. The children easily understood this process and attempted to narrate the story as they reviewed the dialogue. It is clear from the text that they were struggling, in most instances attempting to describe the scene, and in many cases repeating the dialogue. Nevertheless, they were caused to reflect on aspects of language as they attempted to take progressive steps from the embedded dialogue to the more disembedded narrative. As they and many others have experienced, the journey into literacy crosses many a desert. But the Bubble Dialogue tool allowed them to engage in a reflexive process in a sustained manner over an extended period; it was as if they were carrying a water supply on their journey.

Back to the story within our story: as our hero, Stephen, continues his relentless quest to save the hapless Stacy, one possible path takes him in the direction of a crocodile. In the first draft of the story, Stephen quite simply dons his Indiana Jones outfit and kills the crocodile. Encouraging the children to revise this simple scenario proved to be difficult. When however we placed a button (a hot spot on the screen) which linked the frozen moment in the story to a Bubble Dialogue in which 'Stephen comes face to face with a very hungry crocodile' the children readily entered into the reconstruction of Stephen's world and created a dialogue in which Stephen, displaying a greater degree of ingenuity than heretofore, manages to trick the crocodile and escape.

Fig. 8. Bubble Dialogue: Stephen and the Crocodile.

In the meantime, Stacy faces the Monster. In an attempt to cause the children to cast Stacy in a more positive light (we also had our agenda!), this Bubble Dialogue scene was introduced thus: 'The clever Stacy tries to talk to the monster so that he will not eat her.' Although some would question the power of Stacy's strategies in this situation;

> 'If he sets the table I am going to scream'

and

> 'maybe if I say my prise (prayers) somethink will happen.'

others might regard her attempts to divert the monster from his purpose as typical of those deemed to be available to females in our society.

We have found that Bubble Dialogue has provided the children with a scaffolding in which the process of articulating and elaborating the scene can take place; on reading through their scripts, they spontaneously begin to review and redraft their narrative writing. In the review mode, the narration of the story causes the children to engage again in the reflective process. The beginning of the scene is neatly captured, 'Then Stacy looked in the monster eyes and the look on Stacy face was horriefing.'

Fig. 9. Bubble Dialogue: Stephen and the Monster.

The use of the Bubble Dialogue tool was typical of the use made of other tools for literacy which we have under development. Our findings to date are that young children, and less able children too, as in this case, enjoy writing individually and collaboratively within the hypermedia environment using digitised graphics and sound and tools for literacy like the Bubble Dialogue tool. Two other tools, StoryMaker and ProjectMaker, emerged from research undertaken in other classrooms for other purposes and in all cases we found that the tools were effective, provided that teachers were well versed in their use and in the reasons for using them, and provided also that they were used within contexts reflecting the current concerns of the children and within the on-going curriculum.

Most stories have one ending; this one has many

One last point: we forgot to mention that the Stacy and Stephen story has many endings, some happy, some sad. The one we like best happens to incorporate a sound generated, recorded, digitised and installed by the children themselves. Those 'readers' who have heard the crocodile munching Stephen (who in this ending is eaten if he is unlucky enough to fish in the wrong pond) will never forget the experience. The children, whose digitised munching conveys more than is possible with mere words, are only too pleased to see the effect of their 'writing' on their audience.

Our story, too, has several endings. One is clearly unfinished, in that we do not yet know enough about what is happening when children make use of the Bubble Dialogue tool. While we have already experienced and observed the creation of many Bubble Dialogue scripts in many contexts, including the one we have just described, unravelling the complexity of the interactions taking place between the children and the teacher and linking these interactions to those being generated between the screen-based characters are tasks hardly yet addressed, yet alone completed. Nevertheless, we have had enough experience to allow us to come to a broad conclusion, really a conviction arising from extensive classroom experience, which we think is worth noting.

We are convinced that children can make good use of multimedia environments in classrooms, not merely as consumers of packages of information, or whatever, developed outside the classroom, but as developers and communicators in their own right. However, what we call 'good use' is only possible under at least two conditions: when the teacher is well versed in the use of the technology and has been able to see how its use in classrooms integrates with and extends 'normal' good practice and when scaffolding is provided for the teacher and the pupil so that at least their early explorations of multimedia in the classroom can take place within a technological framework tailored to specific educational goals, as in the case we have described here.

Ginny got us into multimedia storying. Her need to talk to a crab got us into Bubble Dialogue. Orla's creations, Kim and Pat, showed us that children and teachers would be likely to gain from using a developed version of Bubble Dialogue in the classroom. Kerry-Ann, Faye and Andrew and Seamus Coyle are typical of the many story-telling children and teachers who, since Orla first opened our eyes to the possibilities, have shown us that we are on at least one of the right tracks.

References

Hardy, B. (1977) Narrative as a primary act of mind. In Meek, M., Warlow,A., Barton, G., *The Cool Web,* Bodley Head, London.
Cohen, L. & Manion, M. (1985) *Research Methods in Education,* Croom Helm, London.

12
Using *HyperCard* in writing narratives

Moira and Richard Monteith

When you read some of the other chapters in this book (for example, those by Stephen Marcus and Harry McMahon) you will understand the revolutionary aspects of hypermedia. This particular computer application may seem light years away from your classroom practice if you are currently one of those 74% with the use of one Acorn BBC B or Master computer in a primary classroom. That statistic comes from the DES Survey of Information Technology in Schools, June 1991 (DES, 1991). The survey also reveals that we are changing practice concerning information technology (IT) very rapidly. More teachers are using computers more often and with greater confidence than in 1988 and 1985. The effects of revolutions have the habit of creeping up on us more quickly than we think. The National Curriculum requires us to draw young children's attention to the highly computerised nature of the world in which we live (National Curriculum, 1990), a feature that even a few years ago many teachers would not have focused on within the classroom. Similarly you may find surprisingly soon that you will be using a computer with Hypermedia facilities, probably using a program such as *Guide* for the PC, *HyperCard* for the Macintosh or *Genesis* for the Archimedes. If you have already used one of these programs then our experience may help you to extend your use of such applications or that of your pupils or students.

One of the major benefits of using this type of software is the freedom it gives to link material from different media: for example, illustration, text, sound and video to provide a kind of electronic collage. A conventional collage is static and cannot be changed readily once the parts have been pasted onto it. This collage is dynamic and can be changed or edited as items can easily be added, moved to a different location or removed altogether either by the original creators or subsequent readers. Moreover, the items themselves can be dynamic, for example, video clips. Links can be made between elements such as single words or phrases or individual picture images and other relevant material. Thus a reader, by clicking on a single word or part of an illustration, can move automatically to information about it. Daniel Chandler suggested as long ago as 1985 (Chandler *et al.*,1985) that we might be moving forwards into an era of literacy comparable in some ways to that of the middle ages where manuscripts were illustrated and their production was often a collaborative, co-operative venture. Individual authorship was not an important ingredient and became so only when printing was widespread. We believe that hypermedia lend themselves even more than previous computer applications to collaborative ventures.

Such collaboration may involve more than the three or four users developing a project together. It may include others who have created previous material and resources, including the software, used in the project. One individual might put a stack together but she might use material available from other resources such as museums or work created by other authors and now out of copyright. Many such stacks have been developed such as the one by Stuart Lee on World War 1 poets, using material from the Imperial War Museum[1]. In terms of classroom use, the evidence of a project that used to adorn the walls for a few months until it became too dusty can now be retained as long as it is useful. So, for example, a project on transport created by three 13 year olds can be looked at by members of another class another year. They could add different sections and improve or correct any of the information contained within the stack if they so wished, or they could create their own version, thus optimising the learning possibilities available to them.

Why these projects?

We chose to look at three different ages in the school continuum to see if *HyperCard* as used on Macintosh computers could be a useful tool for teachers throughout the age range. We also wanted to find out if it could be used reasonably easily as there is no point in trying to persuade teachers to use computer software that presents a number of operational difficulties. We were also curious to try out different versions of projects we had attempted before using other software or work we had seen developed elsewhere.

We had admired Harry McMahon's work tremendously and wanted to see if we could replicate the kind of project he and Bill O'Neill have undertaken. They have immense ability at communicating and perhaps the system would not work without their talents. We decided to work therefore with a class in an infants school to see how feasible a *HyperCard* approach would be. We wanted the children to draw pictures and use these as a basis for developing their own conversations and narratives, to see if they could use the resources easily and if was possible for someone - perhaps a parent or secondary school pupil on work experience - to oversee this task using a template form built up by the teacher.

We had worked with branching narratives with both junior and secondary school pupils. In particular we had used *Storytree*, devised and produced by Derbyshire LEA for the BBC microcomputer (an account of which was included in

---

[1] Further information about this stack can be obtained from Stuart Lee, CTI Centre for Textual Studies, Oxford University Computing Service.

IT's English, (1988)), and *LINX 88,* produced by the Prolog in Education group[2] . We found the structure of branching narratives particularly useful in focusing pupils' attention on the nature of plots and also, by encouraging alternative routes to the story line, ensuring that pupils did not finish off characters for a dramatic ending, often by violent means. They had to consider alternatives within the plot structure and alter characters' actions and motivation accordingly.

Redrafting need not focus solely on the improvement of individual texts. Children and beginning writers can consider the development of characterisation, plot and use of setting over a number of their own texts. They can alter point of view, move from first person narrative to third (and vice versa) and even change the form, from short story to play, for example. Clarity of expression and a developing ability to convey the meaning the writer intends are also important concerns and pupils can work on these communicative aspects as they focus on different lines of the narrative or topic.

Storytree, by its nature and the amount of writing visible on the screen, tended to encourage brief episodes. This brevity worked well in specific instances, such as students writing stories for very young children, but did not allow individual writers much scope. Similarly, *LINX*, often used for linking sequences in history or humanities projects on topics such as Medieval Medicine, tended to allow only brief sections for writing. The secondary pupils with whom we used the program were enthusiastic, writing extra sections unasked, but seemed channelled by the program into episodic narratives in which the characters continually got into and out of difficult situations. This seemed to be how they viewed their own, distinctly compartmentalised, lives: home and often work before school, next their class tutor session, then one lesson after another interspersed with sessions in the playground, home and often a recurring set of problems or challenges there. One group wrote about describing their education to the alien occupants of a spaceship. 'The teacher demands more facts "I want more facts or you'll regret it." You feel frightened. You try to think of more facts quickly. "Mr Hull is our Headteacher, there are 600 pupils in our school". As you look round the table you see all the aliens are laughing at you.' Another group wrote: 'You pass the space history class and then there are corridors leading to different subjects, a corridor for Maths, a corridor for English a corridor for PE. You pass through the corridor to some kind of a space dome and meet some strange looking people who ask you to go with them. They take you to a room where there are doctors. They ask you to step into a machine which looks like an X-Ray machine'. Their writing reflected a positive attitude for seeking solutions or ways out of difficulties, perhaps simplistic but nevertheless potential solutions, but the program by its nature precluded much individual writing development. There were also some difficulties in altering the 'choices' that led to different routes. Our logbook indicates that pupils talked and wrote themselves into alternatives which often needed changing subsequently. Writers need to be able to make alterations at

---

2   Further information about LINX and the Prolog in Education group can be obtained from Jon Nichol, Education Department, Exeter University.

any point in their text so we needed to find a software package that would accommodate redrafting. We decided to use *HyperCard* to produce a branching narrative program that would allow episodic plotting but also individual development of particular scenes and settings, illustrations and information.

Thirdly, we wanted to see if we could encourage secondary school pupils to produce an annotated version of a text such as that developed by Dr Des O'Brien as part of the Stella Project at Glasgow University. He has edited William Langland's poems so that readers can move easily from a text to a translation to notes to a glossary and so on. We decided to see if pupils could develop a similar version of Chaucer's *Prologue*. Subsequently we widened our objectives after discussion with teachers at the school involved.

Software development

HyperCard on the Apple Macintosh was our choice for the three pilot projects we undertook to explore the potential of hypermedia for the classroom. We used the software rather like a construction kit. It enables users to build a coherent structure called a stack from pieces, both text and pictures, that they have produced themselves or obtained from other sources and wish to incorporate with their own material.

For each group with which we worked our aim was to produce an empty stack with card layout specially designed to receive the material produced by the pupils and to display it in a way appropriate to their particular project. The stacks had to be simple enough to use without an extensive knowledge of *HyperCard* while not placing any unnecessary restrictions on the users' actions. We wanted the users to be able to concentrate on what they were doing without having to worry unduly about how to do it. In the stacks we created pupils and staff needed only to use simple computer skills: to enter text, draw on screen and click buttons. By using *HyperCard*'s programming facilities we have been able to automate virtually all the other operations required in the construction of a stack. Pupils and staff were free to plan and concentrate on creative and imaginative processes without having to continually consider whether or not they were at the correct *HyperCard* level or how to create and place a new button and link it to another card.

In the case of the first project the task was straightforward. Each pupil drew a character directly onto a card and we then added a speech bubble. Several copies of the card were made so that the pupils could type in a dialogue sequence. The only computer skills required were the ability to use *HyperCard*'s tool palette to draw or type on the screen and the six-year-old pupils rapidly became very adept at these tasks. The only special software facility added to this stack was an ability to construct a story from the individual finished cards. Clicking on an 'Edit' button enabled us to select in order the cards required for an individual narrative. Once this had been done a 'Read' button appeared on the first page. Clicking this button hid it and all other buttons on the screen, the reader had then only to click the mouse to proceed to each subsequent page of the story. Once you have the cards in the order you wish, you could just move from one to the other by pressing the arrow key.

Our second project involved the pupils in the production of branching narratives with illustrations. This requires the facility to link one card to one or several other cards. Each of the story pages in this stack, which we have named *Storytrail*[3], has a scrolling text field into which text can be entered. In this way we were able to circumvent the limitations of the restricted length of text inherent in the programs we had previously used. If a page is required for an illustration, clicking the 'Draw' button removes the text field from the card and reveals the tool palette. Illustrations or diagrams are then added directly to the card either by using the tool palette or by pasting imported material. Links are established from text pages by clicking the 'Add Links' button. The user is then offered the choice of establishing up to six links from a page. When the number chosen is clicked, the appropriate number of buttons is automatically created and placed on the page. These buttons can be linked to other pages by clicking the 'Link to' button.

The third group of pupils undertook the project on Chaucer's *Prologue*. We needed to link individual words in this project rather than link pages as in *Storytrail*. Such a facility is not built into *HyperCard* currently but we were able to program it into a stack we named *Keylinks*. This stack consists of three types of pages: text, illustration and glossary. Text and illustration pages are similar to those in *Storytrail* except that text pages have a second scrolling field listing linked words. So for instance, the words 'Tabard Inn' were listed in the Chaucer stack because they were linked to another page of additional notes which the reader might wish to peruse. Unusual or archaic words in the text were listed in the same way as they were linked to the glossaries made by the pupils. Forming linkages using words instead of buttons is an extremely simple process. The user simply selects a word and clicks on it while holding down the Shift Key and entering the number of the page selected for the link. Once a link has been formed in this way, clicking on the word with the mouse will take the reader to the linked page. If this page is a glossary page the program will find and highlight the occurrence of this word on the page, automatically scrolling down the page if necessary to do so.

Ecclesall: the development of an illustrated narrative

The children, all aged from six years to six years and three months, worked with us in pairs or threes. Usually they spent 20 minutes or so at the computer at one time so this activity was included within the range of activities undertaken by class members. The computer, a Mac-Plus, was placed on one of the tables so that children working elsewhere frequently passed by and commented on the work currently on screen. The class teacher selected the pairs of children to work with us. All had

---

3   Further information about this software can be obtained from Richard Monteith.

made some progress in reading but only one group of three girls could read with any ease. They had all used a BBC computer previously but had not word-processed any text. They were familiar only with a limited number of keys used for specific packages. A few who had computers at home said they used them for playing games and drawing pictures.

Each group had three or more usually four sessions at the computer, so roughly spent an hour and 20 minutes each in total. By the end of this time they had produced enough material to make up a small book. During the first session they drew a character on the screen using the toolbox in *HyperCard*. The children appeared to have little trouble using the mouse and their manipulation of the drawing tools improved rapidly. First of all they were shown how to use the pencil or paintbrush and the eraser. After about ten minutes of this warm-up activity each drew their character, often an animal or insect.

Before the second session we used the circle from the tool palette to draw a 'speech circle' near the characters so they looked as if they were thinking or speaking. All the children recognised this convention. They thought up a greeting which they then typed in the empty space. We asked them in pairs or threes to think up a conversation between the characters. We wrote this down on a piece of paper as they were talking. Here are examples of two of the scripts.

1. Wilfred (an ant), Susie (a cat) and Domino (a rabbit)

Wilfred (says):	**Let's go into the garden and play on the swings.**
Susie (says):	**Yes, I will come on the swings.**
Domino (says):	**I will come too.**
Wilfred (thinks):	I'm going to like it.
Susie (thinks):	I'll like it too.
Domino (thinks):	It's going to be good.
Wilfred (says):	**The sun is shining.**
Susie (says):	**I'd like to play in the sun.**
Domino (says):	**I want to hide in the hay.**
Wilfred (thinks):	I'll go on the swings, you can go and play in the sun.
Susie (thinks):	Yes, I will like it.
Domino (thinks):	I think I will hide in the hay from the sun.

2. Two boys; Smiley and Matthew

Smiley (says):	**Good morning**
Matthew (says):	**Do you want to come to my house one day?**
Smiley (thinks):	I think he's got Thundercats.
Matthew (thinks):	He might come.

Smiley (says):	**Yes, I will come to your house on Friday.**
Matthew (says):	**Yes, we'll play at football.**
Smiley (thinks):	Well, he might not have them.
Matthew (thinks):	I'm pleased.

The children typed in their script during sessions three and four, using the text tool. If they made a mistake they had to rub it out - an activity unfortunately they enjoyed, often rubbing out words for the sake of it. They did have some difficulty at first in finding the letters on the keyboard but clearly improved very quickly. We had no doubt that if they were able to use a keyboard frequently they would have little trouble in entering text. Booklets were made of their text and the children read them to the class and took them home to read.

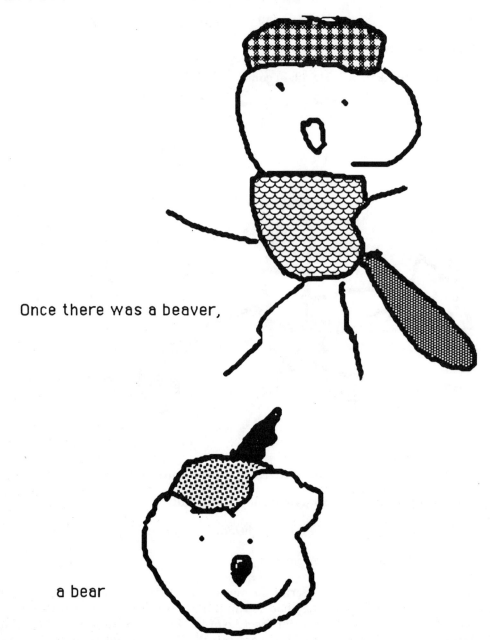

Once there was a beaver,

a bear

and a moose.

The class teacher asked us if a group of three girls could do a second story which would be a version of a class story centred around three characters. It was clear from the drawings made in their second story that the girls had improved in confidence and wished to progress further. They made three sets of drawings for this story, and evidently wished to use more tools and experiment further. For instance, they took an oblong shape to depict a scarf and then drew in the fringes. They were also more particular about details. The moose's sledge was very precisely drawn and each line indicated a specific part of the sledge as visualised by the artist. They developed the story line adroitly, even introducing a problem before the successful conclusion. 'They couldn't find a shop that sold a hat, a scarf, a sledge and a coat. They kept on walking and they found the right shop.'

Conclusions

After discussion with the class teacher we agreed that such a project would be viable in a classroom situation. The teacher would spend as much time as she felt was possible discussing the children's dialogue outline with them. The remainder of the work could be organised with the support of anyone else who helped in the classroom, for instance a student or parent. Providing pupils with challenging work with a computer is arguably preferable to allowing children to use the computer unsupervised, as often happens. It then becomes important to consider what the challenging work is going to be.

In this project the children developed expertise with the keyboard, mouse and printer. More importantly they used direct, vigorous prose to convey their ideas, often with two- or three-way interaction which allowed sophisticated understanding of nuance and intention not usually observed or developed in other class writing. A visiting HMI commented specifically on the way the subtleties of the pupils' command of language was both encouraged and illustrated by their writing here.

Walkley: the branching structure approach to collaborative writing

Five groups, each of three children, collaborated in this activity. They came mostly from one class of ten- to eleven-year-olds but three were younger and from another class. The whole school had just completed a project on 'Old Walkley' so we built on this initiative. We started each group of three children with the same paragraph which described starting off to school one fine morning. Each group chose a time span in which their narratives occurred: Walkley in the time of the dinosaurs, the Victorian age, at the time of the Sheffield Flood, during World War 2 and at some unidentified time in the future. All the children spent time researching the background to their narratives, usually drawing on material they had used in previous projects. They wrote some sections collaboratively, some individually, but all straight into the computer. Unfortunately there was little time for much in the way of redrafting though such an activity would be feasible in a general classroom situation.

The illustrations were varied. Two boys drew a map of the Sheffield Flood extremely rapidly, in 20 minutes, straight on the screen. One revealed quite brilliant draughtsmanship in selecting features from a more detailed map we had found and calculating the scale needed. With only one computer there was no time for each group to use it for their illustrations. Therefore their drawings on paper were scanned onto cards and integrated within the narrative. In this way their illustrations became an important feature of the text rather than a separate entity. We also considered the requirements of potential readers. In the 'read only' version readers could choose their reading pathway, for instance moving from one individual passage to another text to a group text to illustration. A typical list of choices for the reader would be :

𝕸𝖆𝖕 𝖔𝖋 𝖙𝖍𝖊 𝕾𝖍𝖊𝖋𝖋𝖎𝖊𝖑𝖉 𝖋𝖑𝖔𝖔𝖉.

by Scott and Tom

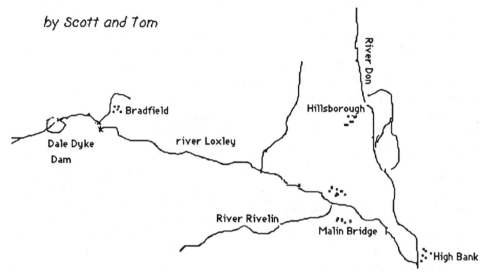

1 Do you go with Scott to Malin Bridge?

2 Do you go with Tom to Hillsborough?

3 Do you go with Katherine to High Bank?

4 Do you want to see the map of the Flood?

Conclusions

Once the initial framework had been agreed, the pupils could get on with their sections unaided, though some pupils needed help to sort out the choices mechanism when they were writing. The software provided an excellent framework for a very diverse set of writing and did not enforce the rather narrow structure of the previous programs we had used. We found that *HyperCard* led to a structure which was extremely flexible as regards multi-author collaboration and reading pathways. This seemed particularly beneficial in that pupils were helped to design structures appropriate for their writing rather than follow one pattern. The overall structure can include factual information as well as a story line and can build on individual strengths as well as collaborative work. Illustrations can become a functional part of the text similar in a way to the function of diagrams.

Projects of this kind depend on interaction away from the computer as well as actually working with it. One of the unforeseen discoveries concerned the significance of topic work to their writing. The children decided on their own 'period', the only proviso being that all groups chose a different time. They chose times around which they had already completed projects. They knew where to find some books and folders that gave them information and they were quite insistent that they should find the details which fitted with their conceptualisation. So, for example, it took quite a long search to find the 'appropriate' dinosaurs. The different research backgrounds led to different narratives, all of which could be accommodated within the structure. The dinosaur encounters tended to be peaceable, evoking scenes of mutual trust and helpfulness, perhaps building on the way young children in general are encouraged to conceptualise animals. The Victorian narrative was the most violent, dealing in particular with teachers punishing pupils. The Sheffield Flood included the longest written episodes, inspired by contemporary pictures of the event showing an amazing collection of debris left by the flood: furniture, horses, cows, long planks of wood and trees all washed together in piles. There was also and perhaps inevitably a picture of a dog rescuing a baby in a cradle. Maybe the visual stimuli here produced the lengthy accounts. Our project did illustrate how formative good topic work can be and how useful it is to exploit this knowledge retrospectively.

The Hope Valley Edition of Chaucer's *Prologue*

As with most English projects, we had multiple aims which were realised in varying degrees with some unexpected results. We had several discussions with the class teacher before beginning the project. Our major aim was to encourage a historical perspective in language use while at the same time introducing Year 9 students in a comprehensive school to Chaucer's *Prologue*. We were concerned to develop students' editing skills at redrafting, compiling, creating and using glossaries and notes. They worked in groups and we asked them to organise their own work as far as possible, move on from one activity to another, divide the work among themselves and to set their targets for each period. In terms of a finished product, we wanted a stack of material on *HyperCard* which we could give other classes or schools to build on if they wished. One of the beauties of *HyperCard* projects, as already mentioned, is their potential for subsequent use and further development. The class also produced a book for the library.

We had the use of two computers usually: a Macintosh Plus with an Imagewriter II printer and external hard disk, and a BBC Master 128. The latter was used only for word-processing and the files were subsequently transferred to the Macintosh through a coupling lead using *VIEWMAC* software. The class were mixed ability with one pupil with special needs. They had worked together as a class for four months but undertaken very little collaborative work. The pupils made their decision to work in friendship, single-sex groups, except for one group which was mixed. Very few had hands-on experience but all responded very favourably to the computers.

Geoffrey Chaucer

The whole class first read a section of Chaucer's *Prologue* where the pilgrims set out from Southwark. They wrote a modern version in groups and then compared versions. After a general discussion about the *Prologue*, they selected one or two characters on which to focus. One group word-processed their version of the start of the pilgrimage while the others began work on their characters, writing on paper. In retrospect, the lack of machines did not matter particularly at this point. We felt that the students gained from discussing their versions with each other and having the printed original in front of them. We had two glossaries the pupils could use and definitely needed half a dozen. We did not provide any modern versions of the text.

Members of staff read aloud the pupils' 'new' versions and duly praised them as they were of a very high quality. Listening to their own translations proved an important stimulus. Each version was word-processed by the group concerned. Subsequently, we suggested editing improvements to remove archaic or stilted language or a mistaken interpretation of Chaucer's meaning. It would have been helpful for all students to work at the computer, but with seven groups and two computers this was not feasible. So they edited their printed-out versions first on paper and then keyed in the alterations in turn.

One group drew an illustration of the Shipman using *MacPaint* software. We had hoped that several groups could draw their character in this manner but, although they were extremely keen, it took up too much time in terms of computer use. Therefore we had to ask students to draw illustrations on paper and subsequently their pictures were transferred to the computer by scanning. Unfortunately the students were unable to see this process as it was carried out away from the classroom; we did not have the equipment available in school.

The groups compiled glossaries, began background notes and wrote introductions to their characters, using library books for extra information. The software allows the reader to move freely through the material and to establish links between individual words and references on other pages or in glossaries. For example, clicking on a keyword in Chaucer's poem could take the reader to the corresponding students' version on another page.

In practical terms, frustration could have been minimised if more machines had been available or, possibly, if two groups had been able to work on the computers during every English lesson. As it was, we had more and more material being produced and, although the pupils also created an exhibition using their drawings and background notes, the mountain of information could not be processed quickly enough.

Nearly all students were enthusiastic about working in groups, though most realised that 'conflicts of ideas were a problem'. One of the most positive features of their comments concerned editing:

Amy:	Hard - but fun. You have to get everything perfect.
David:	I have learnt how to check things over more thoroughly - spellings and paragraphs etc.
Dominic:	I learnt that you needed to edit a piece of work before it is properly finished.
Zachary:	It's quite hard to edit pieces of a book and you have to concentrate.

We were happy to find that Chaucer as writer was not entirely ignored. Kate wrote: 'It's difficult to read, but when you can read it properly you notice that it rhymes.'

Most commented on the factual information they'd learnt about their characters or pilgrimages, or about the difficulties of the language used.

Kate:	It is different and at first hard to read and to tell what it says but after a while it got easier and I thought it was quite a good language but I'd rather still use modern English.
Joe:	I have learnt how different it is, that it contains French and Latin words also.

Bryan, Daniel and Zachary:

> Sounds Frenchy - e's everywhere and y's. It's hard to translate. We change the order of the words he uses.

David, Charlotte and Robert:

> It's a lot different but not tons. The words sound English but not the way they're written. We're getting better at guessing.

Vickie and Fiona: Complicated and hard to pronounce. It makes more sense if you say it aloud.

Encouraging the wide variety of skills involved in editing has become more feasible with the advent of wordprocessing. We discovered the potential is greater with software which allows users to integrate graphics with text. With such technology, a look at literature first presented as an illuminated manuscript seems highly appropriate.

What we have learned from the projects

The teacher has an important organisational role in using hypermedia with pupils or students. The questions that need addressing are different from those customarily prompted by taking up a facilitating role in the classroom or even that of an expert adviser. Training systems using hypermedia are being developed which limit the options almost entirely - for example, one where trainees are learning how to install a house wiring system. In this instance they need to know specific requirements not a list of options. But if we agree with Stephen Marcus that 'A stack might be a great resource for students, but the person who had the most fun and learned the most was probably the person who created it,' then the function of the teacher becomes more to develop and help organise their students' pursuit of knowledge.

Underwood and Underwood ask a pertinent question: 'As programs generally become more user-friendly we will have an increasing population who lack conceptual understanding of the processes they are involved in. Does this matter? To the purist of course it does, the IT goal is lost, but pragmatically perhaps it does not' (Underwood & Underwood, 1990). Programs such as *HyperCard* encourage sophisticated learning approaches where the skill input is not a matter of computer based knowledge, either in terms of programming or manipulating complicated software. The skills involved are the traditional ones concerned with curricular organisation. The teacher necessarily is concerned with the framework of learning, for instance, particular objectives for Keystage 3 of the National Curriculum. However, the pupils need to decide the requirements of their hypermedia file, whether it is a record, a revision aid or a guide for someone else to learn or read or profit by in some way. They need to determine what information should be included and where they can gain the requisite information.

This kind of expert use of knowledge may well encourage a new learning approach. Clearly people need to learn facts; apart from anything else we enjoy remembering them and giving opinions on them. However, we do need help in finding structures to place these facts efficiently. It is no good proving to students how biased their reading or information sources may be unless they can counter this limitation in some way. The significant features of these new technological tools allow students and pupils to construct alternative structures, make their own training designs, build upon what they have already queried and tested. If pupils are encouraged to consider ways of selecting, organising and communicating information throughout their school career they may become as skilful communicators as their early abilities indicate. Their potential is often not realised. As David Wood summarises: 'a significant proportion of adolescents are poor at giving a good account of themselves when asked to inform and explain; unable to exploit their communicative resources to the full' (Wood, 1988). As teachers and learners ourselves, we all know by now the hollowness of any suggestion of a technological fix. Yet it does seem possible that the new technological developments may lead to increased confidence in both using and querying or challenging information. It may well be that these new tools will bring us back to traditional educational goals for the enquiring human mind.

Acknowledgements

We would like to thank the staff and pupils from Ecclesall Infants School, Walkley Middle School and Hope Valley College. We received particular support from Barbara Daniel, Margaret Anderson and Rosa Stevens.

References

Chandler, D. & Marcus, S. (eds.) (1985) *Computers and Literacy*. Milton Keynes, Open University Press.

DES, (1991) *Statistical Bulletin* (June), prepared by the Government Statistical Service and available from the DFE Analytical Services Branch, Mowdem Hall, Staindrop Road, Darlington, County Durham DL3 9BG.

IT's English, (1988 republished 1990) NATE Publication.

National Curriculum, (1990) Programme of study key stage 1, Information Technology capability. DFE London.

Underwood & Underwood, (1990) *Computers and Learning*..Blackwell, Oxford.

Wood, D. (1988) *How Children Think and Learn*. Blackwell, Oxford, p.145

Index